IT PAYS TO

GOD

The Principle of Responding to God

To Mrs S Musendo

Happy Birthday

From Mai Tapa

Reverend Mystery Muzangaza

DEDICATION

This book is dedicated in memory of the following:

To my late mother, Maria Magore nee Musenha who when I was only 10 years was suddenly promoted to glory, but she had already inculcated in me a sense of responsibility and a love for God.

Oh! What a strong foundation it is? May her soul rest in peace.

To my late father Nyson Chikonobaya Magore who was promoted also to glory in June 1991, but he had taught me already how to pray and to trust in the Lord. To date I am enjoying the fruit of the wonderful teachings.

Thanks dad.

To my late stepmother Naomi Magore nee Chakanya whom the Lord called to rest in peace on 15th November 2017, I thank you for being an excellent mother who taught me great lessons on faith, hope and love in the Lord.

Rest in peace as you take pride in your son whom you raised to be a Pastor.

Lastly, I dedicate this book to God the Father, the Son, and the Holy Spirit who enables me to both will and do according to His divine purpose.

ACKNOWLEDGEMENTS

This book could not have been my first book if in all honesty I had listened and taken advice from my dear, gracious, and lovely wife, Lucy who persistently and on numerous occasions kindly asked me to put in writing what the Lord had done in our family and our ministry as ministers of the gospel. I regrettably owe her my sincere apology for the delay and unnecessary procrastination. I am also very grateful for all her prayers without which I could not have achieved anything.

I am so grateful to my three sons Emmanuel, Theophilus, Timothy, and my two loving daughters-in-love (law) Precious, Margarette, and my two grandsons Ethan and Tinotenda Muzangaza who spared me time to be away from them as I took hours to write this wonderful book.

Certain people are God sent in one's life. They just come into one's life just in time to trigger dormant things. Pastors Ron and Viollah Danda are God sent indeed. They gave me a final hard kick to make me begin to write this book. They persistently checked with me (especially the wife), if I had started the book writing and continuing to write. I will forever be grateful to this couple.

I am grateful to my siblings Nereus, Moses and Zebulun my brothers and Nesta and Tryphena my dear sisters who were my role models, mentors, and from whom I learnt of the love of Jesus Christ and the sweet fellowship of the Holy Spirit.

Members of Harvest of Souls Ministries UK were an inspiration to me in writing this book. Each of them gave me testimonies about God's faithfulness in their lives. From such testimonies, I drew lessons too on trusting in the Lord. A young 18-month kid by the name Mutsawashe Chitanda encouraged my faith in the Lord, when out of his own initiative came to kneel before me several times during church services and raised up his hands for me to pray for him. He believed in God and even to this day, he sings songs of praise in church. I will forever be grateful to this church and its membership.

I was born and bred in the Apostolic Faith Mission in Zimbabwe, and I was seconded as a missionary to the United Kingdom to work with the sister church The Apostolic Faith Mission International Ministries UK in 2004 -2017. All my pastoral experiences and testimonies that I shall cite in this book were born in this church. I am who I am through this church by the grace of God. I am grateful to the church leadership and the faithful followers.

Above all, praise and honour belong to the Godhead - the Father, the Son and the Holy Spirit who made the writing of this book a reality by giving me inspiration and revelation.

CONTENTS

SECTION 1: TRUST IS EARNED

Chapter 1: I Just Sneezed

My late father Nyson Muzangaza Magore, (nicknamed Chikonobaya *(meaning a bull that fights viciously)* because no one could withstand his blows when he was fighting if anyone dared to provoke him to anger) named me Mystery a few days after I was born by my late mother Maria Magore nee Musenha.

When people ask me, "What is your name"? and I tell them, "Mystery"; they normally take a deep breath, throw a smile at me in amazement and then repeat, Mystery? as if to doubt my name and some with keen interest, do probe why my parents called me Mystery.

Indeed, I am a mystery. My birth was a mystery. My growth was a mystery. My life is a mystery. My calling as a gospel minister was a mystery. It's a mystery to serve the Lord Jesus Christ. It's a mystery what I will be in eternity. Everything of me is just a mystery.

When all hope is gone and a dark, thick cloud of misery overshadows you and no other man is there to stand with you and console you; my parents learnt that it pays to put your trust in the Lord with all your heart and never at any time to lean on your understanding but to simply commit all your ways unto Him, the author of life.

I am Mystery because my parents as devout Christians believed in God and trusted in God with all their hearts. My parents learnt one great lesson through me, that it pays to trust in the Lord.

It was on a certain Wednesday in April 1958, in the village of Muzangaza under Chief Negomo in Chiweshe rural area in Zimbabwe that certain Christian women of the Apostolic Faith Mission in Zimbabwe (then of South Africa and hereinafter AFM in Zimbabwe) were midwives to help my mother deliver me, not at a clinic or hospital but in a rural hut with soot on the roof. My birth brought joy to my mother since she had previously lost a healthy three-month baby boy under mysterious circumstances. This was not the reason why my parents called me Mystery.

On Friday, my father who was a lorry driver and a peasant farmer too came from the capital city of Harare, Zimbabwe (then Salisbury, Rhodesia) to a surprise and good news that my mother had given him another baby son. I am told that they knelt on their knees and thanked God for such a wonderful gift to the family. After a joyful weekend on a Monday, he left for work back to Harare until the next Friday.

Born a Wednesday, the following Wednesday something tragic happened while my dad was away at work in Harare and my mum was alone with me. It was exactly one week after my birth when suddenly, all grapes turned sour. In no time, I was told; I had a hot temperature and I started gasping for air and within no time, I had opened wide a white eye and lifeless. Guys, I had breathed my last breadth. I was dead.

My mother, Maria, a great woman of faith, just like the woman of Shunem in the Bible (2Kings 4:20-23) who had a son who had died suddenly did not disclose to anyone what had happened. My death had followed consecutively a previous sudden death of my two-month elder brother whom I came after. This was a great toll

4

to a lone woman, and she could not withstand the grief, pain and sorrow. She immediately took me to our local resident Pastor, the late Reverend Nyanzira of AFM in Zimbabwe who lived a little distance away from our home.

I am told that my mother when she arrived at the Pastor's residence, sobbing her eyes in tears, she left me into his hands. She said, "If my son does not come back to life again after you have prayed, please, let your wife bury him where I would not know". (The Pastor's wife was one of the rural traditional midwives who had helped my mother to deliver me).

In the Zezuru culture, when a baby dies within a month of its birth, it is buried by older women of the village in a clay vessel by the riverbanks in the absence of its mother. This was the reason why my mother told the pastor such words as she left to go back home. She neither went back nor enquired of me if I was buried since she left me in the Pastor's hands.

It was a mystery. The Pastor failed to understand how a woman can bring a dead child only to leave it in his hands with instructions to bury it, if the child does not come back to life again. Thankfully, the Pastor was a man of prayer and a man who trusted in the

He was a man who believed that all things are possible to him who believes in the Lord.

Lord. He was a man with a violent faith – a faith that can move mountains. What else could he have done at that moment in time with a dead child in his hands except to pray?

As a Pastor he had been teaching his congregation on the power of prayer and the need of having faith in God. I am told that he had been teaching his congregation about the God kind of faith as stated in Mark 11:22-24.

"And Jesus answered them, "Have faith in God. Truly, I say to you, whoever says to this mountain, be taken up and thrown into the sea,' and does not doubt in his heart, but believes that what he says will come to pass, it will be done for him. Therefore, I tell you, whatever you ask in prayer, believe that you have received it, and it will be yours".

Now tables had turned upside down. The teacher had become the student to sit his examination paper and prove himself that he can pass. The dead baby, as an examination paper was right at his table, as he lay dead in his hands.

The Pastor took me, dead as I was to the nearby mountain called Dambo to pray. He carried nothing with him except me wrapped in the baby towel. He had no food and no milk with him since the baby was dead. He went to the top of the mountain and laid me by a bush. He went few meters (yards) away from me and fell down to his knees, face down and between his knees to pray. He prayed without ceasing, night and day from Wednesday until late Friday afternoon.

A one-week-old dead child was up the mountain, wrapped in a towel, the pastor praying for three days without ceasing. The Pastor had no time to eat since he had carried no food and it was not a time of luxury. Eating is a luxury. You eat when things are okay. In moments of grief and pain, it's quite difficult to get an appetite for food. He was praying for a resurrection miracle. He had vowed never to come down the mountain unless the baby was alive again. He trusted in the Lord. He did not lean on his understanding that the child was dead. He did not lean on his understanding that what will people say that he was doing with a dead child in the mountain for three days. He simply believed and trusted in the Lord.

On the third day, on a late Friday afternoon, while kneeling on his feet with his face between his knees, he heard just a sneeze. He stopped praying, and he heard another sneeze. He immediately jumped and ran to this baby that was just now sneezing. He held me in his hands, and *I just sneezed* a third time in his hands. I began to open wide my eyes which he had closed, and I began to move my lips wanting to suck milk from my mother's breast. I was like Lazarus in John chapter eleven in the bible who had come back to live after four days being dead.

Hallelujah! The baby had come back to life again after three days without eating. The Pastor rushed to come down the mountain to his wife so that she could make the baby some very thin watery porridge of mealie meal. As he came down the mountain, my father had just arrived home from Harare. He did not see the baby home with its mother and so he asked, " *Where is the baby"?* He was told by my mother that she did not know whether I was not yet buried for she had left me dead in the Pastor's hands.

Immediately, my parents left for the Pastor's home. As they were just entering the Pastor's courtyard from one direction, the Pastor was arriving at the courtyard in another direction, and they coincidentally met at the entrance to the roof thatched kitchen hut. With a face beaming with a broad smile of a victorious man, the Pastor gave my mother the baby to give it breastfeeding milk.

My father could not understand the story that he was told, and no one had a clear story of what had happened. It was like a fiery tale story. But the evidence was there. God had raised back to life the baby. My father said, "I don't understand this. This is a mystery. Could it be that the baby was dead and never sucked milk for three days and after a fervent prayer of a righteous man, just sneezed? This is a miracle in a million times". So, my father took his holy bible and read about the mysteries of God. He said, "This is none other than the mystery of God and he said the child shall be called Mystery (Chishamiso in my vernacular language meaning the hidden things of God).

The Lord preserved and restored this young baby because he had greater plans with this baby in his kingdom. This is the baby that God called into ministry as a Pastor and now I am the Founder and Senior Pastor of Harvest of Souls Ministries UK. The devil had wanted to bring pain, grief and misery upon my parents and family, but God is faithful. The devil wanted to terminate my life and shutter all the plans of God in my life, but God is faithful.

If I had not just sneezed, the late Reverend Nyanzira could have remained in the mountain until I had decomposed because he was determined never to come back home with a dead baby.

If I had not just sneezed, my parents could have been devastated in their spirits because they could have lost two baby boys in succession while they were still infants.

If I had not just sneezed, I could not have grown up to be a husband, father, pastor, and granddad.

If I had not just sneezed, I could not today be a Founder and Senior Pastor of Harvest of Souls Ministries UK, a church whose mission is to win lost souls for the Kingdom of God.

If I had not just sneezed, I could not have been at this stage of writing a book about trusting in the lord.

If I had not just sneezed, God's plans could have been shuttered. But thanks be to the living God and the Father of our Lord and Saviour Jesus Christ that I just sneezed.

I just sneezed because God wanted to preserve my life. I just sneezed because God wanted me to do great exploits for his kingdom. I just sneezed because God wanted to preserve me so that

I may do His will for the rest of my life. I just sneezed because at that point, I had not started God's agenda for my life.

The Lord preserved my life so that I might be an asset and not a liability in his divine kingdom.

I love the Lord with all my heart, and I do serve him willingly because I know He preserved and restored my life for this very purpose that I should be a minister of the gospel of Jesus Christ. When you see me serve the Lord with all my heart, don't envy me; don't be jealous; don't fight against me; I have come from far, and I have an assignment with the Lord.

I just sneezed so that I may live to do His divine will and not my will. I am not a Pastor by the will of men for men but by the will of Jesus Christ my Lord and my Saviour. When I say, Lord and Saviour, I know what I am saying. My mind will quickly go back to that day when I just sneezed, and my parents said, "it was a mystery" and they called me Mystery.

My parents trusted in the Lord and that is the reason why my mum took me lifeless to the pastor. Our pastor had great faith in God and that is the reason why he took me alone to the mountain to pray until God was able to restore my life. Faith makes all things possible. I am a testimony that faith makes all things possible with God. Through faith or trust in the Lord, God can preserve life.

Hebrews 11:6 says, *"But without faith, it is impossible to please him: for he that comes to God must believe that he is, and that he is a rewarder of them that diligently seek him".*

Mark 11:22-24 *"And Jesus answering said unto them, Have faith in God. For verily I say unto you, that whosoever shall say unto this mountain, be removed, and be cast into the sea; and shall not doubt in his heart but shall believe that those things which he said shall come to pass; he shall have whatsoever he said. Therefore, I say unto you, whatever things you desire, when you pray, believe that you will receive them, and you shall have them".*

I understand why Proverbs 3:5 says, *"Trust in the Lord with all your heart and lean not on your understanding. In all your ways acknowledge the Lord and He shall direct your paths".* If anyone trusts in the Lord, the Lord will be faithful to the request of anyone who trusts in Him. God is the rewarder of those who diligently seek him as stated in Heb. 11:6. By faith, the late Rev Nyanzira saw the mountain of death being removed and cast away into the sea and here I am, fit and strong and ministering the gospel. Oh! what a mystery, as my name is? It pays to trust in the Lord.

As the scripture says, the pastor believed in God when he took me to the mountain, and he received me back from God in the mountain. Apart from the Lord Jesus Christ, I can also say, I was resurrected on the third day by the Lord in the mountain through fervent prayers of a righteous man, the late Reverend Nyanzira.

James 5:16 says, *"... The effectual fervent prayer of a righteous man avails much".* Never at any time should we underestimate the power of prayer, especially, by a righteous person. Think of Elijah and Elisha the prophets of God when they prayed earnestly to the Lord; something always happened. It pays to trust in the Lord. I believe with all my heart that I just sneezed, so that I could be alive today, to write this book, and encourage people amid a global pandemic, to put their trust in the Lord.

Chapter 2: The Deadly Coronavirus (Covid-19)

I was young and now I am more than six decades old, and yet, I had not experienced in my life what the world experienced since the year 2020. At beginning of 2020, we welcomed news from around the world of a rapid spread of a very deadly virus supposedly spreading from Wuhan, China and it was called coronavirus, codenamed COVID-19. Within a short space of time from the attack of the virus, people were dying at very alarming rates. Later, new variants of the virus began to emerge, and they were more deadly than COVID-19.

It was being reported that nobody understood the nature of the virus or disease. There was neither a cure nor a vaccine for the deadly disease. People that were affected were advised to isolate and stay at home and never to visit a clinic, surgery, or hospital. Many died in their homes. Those who managed to reach the hospital died from lack of cure and/or lack of oxygen ventilators. Life was at stake.

It was at this time that I, as a minister of the gospel was left with a challenge to comfort and strengthen the people who were finding no help from nowhere. I was supposed to give a message of hope to the hopeless. It was

The Holy Spirit began to give me a message that "now is the time that the just shall live by faith".

just faith in the Lord that was going to be the people's strengths. People were to learn to trust in the Lord with all their hearts and never to lean on their understanding.

The World Health Organization (WHO) declared the outbreak of a "2019 novel coronavirus (2019-nCoV)" a Public Health Emergency of International Concern on 30 January 2020, and a pandemic on 11 March 2020. In March 2020 after the WHO declaration, countries began to declare national lockdowns where industries, aviation and the shipping came to a halt with no business. The news brought panic and fear to the people. Almost everyone felt vulnerable and hopeless as news continued to be streamed on all TV channels across the globe. The message of Proverbs 3:5 began to resonate with our worldly situation.

> *"Trust in the LORD with all your heart, and do not lean on your own understanding. In all your ways acknowledge him, and he will make straight your paths"* *(Proverbs 3:5).*

On the 16th of March 2020, the virus had already hit the shores of Great Britain where I am domicile, and countless deaths were already taking place with alarming figures being reported by the media outlets daily. On this date, 16th March 2020, Mr Boris Johnson, the British Prime Minister (PM) made a surprise televised statement to the nation saying, "now is the time for everyone to stop non-essential (physical) contact" due to the rapid spreading of COVID-19. He gave the statement as "advice" but with a "very draconian measure".

On the 23rd of March 2020, the same PM addressed the nation and said, "From this evening, I must give the British people a very simple instruction – stay at home". People were advised to leave their homes when it was absolutely essential and for "very limited purposes" such as shopping for necessities, doing one form of physical exercise a day or travel for work if that could not be done from home. Further, gatherings of more than two people from different households in public were banned as well as social events including weddings and religious worship gatherings. The Police were given powers to enforce the rules. That evening, the United Kingdom went into an official national lockdown.

It was like darkness had engulfed the nation with no glimpse of light and hope. I felt in my spirit that I should encourage my fellow Christians to trust in the Lord for protection and for wisdom in knowing what to do and how to apply the prescribed National Healthcare Services (NHS) guidelines and to build our faith in God.

What followed thereafter is catastrophic and a nightmare to nations worldwide as the COVID-19 death toll figures were soaring high in thousands every day. There was no cure, no scientific understanding of the disease and no vaccine yet developed to combat the deadly pandemic. Hospitals were outstretched to capacity with inadequate ventilators for those in need of oxygen and beds were in short supply too.

At this time, as many were losing their loved ones to the pandemic and no medical help seemed to be available globally, people across the globe began to turn their hearts and their cries to the Lord God. In some nations, Christians irrespective of denominations took themselves to the public streets to cry out and call unto God for mercy, healing, the discovering of vaccines and finding a cure for this deadly pandemic.

When I began to see Christians in some parts of the globe take themselves to the streets to cry out to God and pray, I felt the confirmation in my spirit that God will hear the prayers of those that trust in Him, and He will give us protection and the help our medical scientists needed to discover a vaccine and a cure. My message to trust in the Lord was reinforced within me and I was convinced that I should write a book to encourage my fellow brothers and sisters in the Lord.

2 Chronicles 7:13-14 became my inspiration, *"If I shut up heaven that there be no rain, or if I command the locusts to devour the land, or if I send pestilence among my people; If my people, who are called by my name, shall humble themselves, and pray, and seek my face, and turn from their wicked ways; then will I hear from heaven, and will forgive their sin, and will heal their land"*.

Proverbs 3:5-6, *"Trust in the LORD with all your heart; and lean not unto your own understanding. In all your ways acknowledge him, and he shall direct your paths"*.

> It was a call to commit all our ways unto the Lord and not to lean on our understanding.

As I began to meditate upon the two scriptures, it became clearer that these scriptures resonated with the Christians of the 21st century that were facing this deadly pestilence codenamed COVID-19. It was a divine call to Christians across the globe to humble themselves and pray to Jehovah God for mercy and healing of the lands from the deadly pestilence. Christians were to believe and trust in the Lord to heal us from the pandemic. The Lord only was to be our shield and hope during the crisis while we were to take any reasonable precautionary measures as we were being advised by our governments. It was God who was going to help the scientists to discover the vaccine and the possible cure of the deadly pestilence. So, I had this urge in my spirit to encourage the saints to pray, trusting in the Lord to help our scientists to find a vaccine and a cure for COVID-19.

In Numbers 21:4-9, there is an account of when the people had sinned against God, and they were hit by a deadly pestilence. They were being bitten by fiery serpents and they were dying in large numbers and so they cried unto the Lord through Moses. The Lord God told Moses that the only antidote was "make you a fiery serpent and set it upon a pole: and it shall come to pass, that everyone that is bitten when he looks upon it, shall live" (Number 21:8).

Just as those who believed and acted in faith as declared by Moses, lived; so, all the people faced with the COVID-19 and were to trust in the Lord to be protected and saved from the deadly pestilences. The same God who brought an antidote for the fiery serpents and an end to the fiery serpents is the same God who was going to bring healing to our global lands. But this was on the basis that *"If my people, who are called by my name, shall humble themselves, and pray, and seek my face, and turn from their wicked ways; then will I hear from heaven, and will forgive their sin, and will heal their land".*

This Public Health Emergency of International Concern declared as a pandemic on 11 march 2020, should teach us all to trust in the Lord. Brothers and sisters, it pays to trust in the Lord. After people had prayed trusting the Lord to help our scientists develop a vaccine for COVID-19 and to find a cure, BBC News on the bbc.com website dated 8 December 2020, reported that the first women who was to turn 91 years the following week had received her first injection of "Pfizer COVID-19 jab as part of a mass vaccination programme" at 06.31GMT at the University Hospital in Coventry, United

> ◉
> It is the Lord who is going to bring healing to the nations.

> 👁
>
> It pays to trust in the Lord.

Kingdom. Subsequently, other vaccines like Oxford, AstraZeneca vaccine were rolled out in the United Kingdom and other European nations. This was answered prayers of people across the globe who were putting their trust in Lord to help our scientists to find a vaccine and a cure for COVID-19. Death figures began to decline with the rapid rollout of the vaccines in many nations although new variants were being discovered.

Jeremiah 17:7 *"Blessed is the man who trusts in the LORD, whose trust is the LORD.*

Traditionally, vaccines take a long time to be discovered and to pass clinical tests but because of people praying and trusting the Lord, vaccines were quickly discovered and clinically tested and millions across the globe are fully vaccinated against the deadly pandemic. It pays to trust in the Lord.

Chapter 3: Trust Is Earned and Deserved

Biblical evidence clearly shows that God almighty can be trusted because throughout all generations, He earned the trust, and He deserves to be trusted. Having tasted and seen the goodness and faithfulness of the Lord, King Solomon realised that "It Pays to Trust in the Lord". In his wisdom which the Lord had given him without measure, he had to advise his son in Proverbs 3:5 and said,

> *"Trust in the LORD with all your heart, and do not lean on your own understanding. In all your ways acknowledge him, and he will make straight your paths".*

King Solomon was quick to bring to the attention of his son what the Lord is able to do for him if he trusts in the Lord and never leaned on his own understanding. He said, "He will make straight your paths". King Solomon had a recollection of many examples of patriarchs whose paths had been made straight by the Lord.

In his mind, possibly, he had Enoch the seventh-generation patriarch [Jude 1:14] whom he had been told that *"he walked with the Lord"* for 365 years and God ordered his steps, and he was no more for the Lord God Almighty had taken him away alive.

Gen 5:22-24, *"Enoch walked with God after he fathered Methuselah 300 years and had other sons and daughters. Thus, all the days of Enoch were 365 years. Enoch walked with God, and he was not, for God took him".*

King Solomon possibly in his mind, was thinking of Noah whom he was told that he lived at a time when the imagination of every man was evil before God for, they were all exceedingly wicked [Genesis 6:5-6]. Noah in that wicked generation trusted in the Lord with all his heart and he committed all his ways unto Him as he lived to acknowledge the Lord in everything he did. As a result, Genesis 6:8 said, "But Noah found favour in the eyes of the LORD".

King Solomon, son to a great King David, had learnt from his father that it pays to trust in the LORD. He had seen the victories that God had given to his father and how God had ordered his steps and made him a "man after his own heart". For that reason, he was not hesitant to advise his son to "Trust in the LORD" with all his heart and never to lean on his understanding.

King Solomon's teaching to his son was to demonstrate to his son that God should be trusted by his people and that He deserves the trust for it pays to trust in him.

In a context where many people have a title of honour as Lords, it is imperative for me to quickly define the term "LORD" from a biblical perspective. In the United Kingdom, we have two houses of Parliament that discuss and pass legislation. The upper chamber is the House of Lords, and the lower chamber is the House of Commons. Her Majesty the Queen who is the Head of the United Kingdom often addresses the upper chamber as "My Lords".

It is not in this context that we find the word LORD used in the bible. The Hebrew word יְהֹוָה used for *"Lord"* in Proverbs 3:5 is *"Yehovah/Jehovah"* meaning the *eternal and self-existing* most Supreme Being. Above Him, there is none other and never shall there be any other.

Deuteronomy 10:17 says, "For the LORD your God is God of gods, and Lord of lords, a great God, mighty, and awesome, who regards not persons, nor takes reward".

If He is a great God, mighty and awesome. It means that He is worthy to be trusted for everything.

So, a transliteration of Proverbs 3:5-6 would be *"Trust in the eternal and self-existing most Supreme Being, [the God of gods and the Lord of lords, the one who is mighty and awesome] with all your heart, and do not lean on your own understanding. In all your ways acknowledge him, and he will make straight your paths".*

It is clear from the preceding text that the Lord is eternal and self-existing and above Him, there is no other god or lord.

King Solomon's desire was to instil a mindset in his son that "the eternal and self-existing most Supreme Being" earned His trust in generations past and He deserves to be trusted by current generations because He had a credible track record of making paths straight. Unlike the Lords in the Upper Chamber of the United Kingdom Parliament, who at times are found to be untrustworthy and failing; the Sovereign Supreme Being had proved Himself to be reliable, dependable and trustworthy. Isaiah 53:9 says, *"...and there was no deceit in his mouth".*

It is important to note that the desire of the father in Proverbs 3:2 was that the son should prolong his life with many years and that he should prosper. In order to achieve that, there were a few things that the son was encouraged to observe. He was supposed to ensure that:

i.   Love and faithfulness should never leave him.

ii.   He wins the favour of God and the favour of man.

iii. He trusts in the Lord with all his heart.

iv.   He will never lean on his own understanding.

v.   He acknowledges the Lord in all his ways.

vi.   He allows God to make straight his paths.

The key to the longevity of life was trusting in the Lord with all his heart.

He was not supposed to lean on human wisdom/intellect which was equivalent to *"Sophia"* in the Greek language. The reason for trusting in the lord was that he might have a long life full of success. It pays to trust in the Lord.

Brothers and sisters, if anyone is to be trusted in life, he/she should have earned the trust. When people put their trust in you, you should be deserving that trust; for trust is earned and deserved. The LORD earned the trust by the things He did throughout all generations, and He deserves to be trusted.

Chapter 4: Various Perceptions of Trust

While writing this book, I asked several people about what they understood about Proverbs 3:5-6. Their responses were quite interesting, varied and inspiring.

My second daughter-in-law Margorette, said, "It is not an easy scripture to understand and apply in one's own life. It's like you are being asked to put your faith in God when everything else around you don't seem to make sense. It's like you are being asked not to rely upon or depend on your own understanding/intellect but rely on God's understanding of events around you. It's a scripture that teaches us to forget everything that we might know about a situation and focus on what God wants us to do since our ways are not His ways and our thoughts aren't His thoughts, but His ways and thoughts are always perfect".

Well said, my daughter-in-law Margorette. God understands and knows all the events around us. He even knows the end from the beginning. Life exists in Him. He can reveal the future to those who trust in Him and have faith in Him. He can also order their steps to arrive at their intended ending. God always has better plans and thoughts for His people; plans not to harm them but to give them a future and a hope (Jeremiah 29:11). Margorette was not far-fetched in her analysis of the scripture but almost exact. King Solomon wanted his son to put away all confidence in his intellect, wisdom and understanding and rely on the Lord even though everything doesn't seem to make sense around him. This was exactly what well-renowned patriarchs like Abraham, Isaac, Jacob and David had done in their walk with the LORD. These patriarchs had testified by their examples that it pays to trust in the Lord with all your heart. This is one of the reasons why we should trust in the Lord.

Pastor Lucy, my dear wife also said, "Trusting in the Lord is relying or depending upon God for everything; it's committing all your ways unto God. It's refusing to lean on your understanding by trusting in the wisdom of God".

God can be trusted for EVERYTHING.

Oh! What a mouthful statement it is indeed. You can only commit something in someone's care if you trust that person. God is so dependable to such an extent that you can commit all our ways unto Him without suffering any regret. Alleluia!

1 Corinthians 1:25 says, *"For the foolishness of God is wiser than men, and the weakness of God is stronger than men".*

That being the case, the LORD deserves to be trusted with all our hearts. Men built Jericho as an example of a strong, fortified city with iron gates that cannot be destroyed. But God in His 'foolishness' asked the children of Israel to go around the city once every day for seven days.

Joshua 6:9-11 says, *"The armed men were walking before the priests who were blowing the trumpets, and the rear guard was walking after the ark, while the trumpets blew continually. But Joshua commanded the people, "You shall not shout or make your voice heard, neither shall any word go out of your mouth, until the day I tell you to shout. Then you shall shout."* So, he caused the ark of the LORD to circle the city, going about it once. And they came into the camp and spent the night in the camp.

Joshua 6:15-16, *"On the seventh day they rose early, at the dawn, and marched around the city in the same manner seven times. It was only when they had marched around the city seven times, the priests blowing the trumpets that Joshua said to the people, "Shout, for the LORD has given you the city".*

Joshua 6:20, *"So the people shouted, and the trumpets were blown. As soon as the people heard the sound of the trumpet, the people shouted a great shout, and the wall fell down flat, so that the people went up into the city, every man straight before him, and they captured the city".*

The strong, fortified walls came down with a loud shout without any massive artillery being used. It pays to trust in the LORD.

Dr Harriet Saziya, a medical practitioner gave me a personal testimony during the COVID-19 pandemic, and she said, "In the medical profession we rely on scientific evidence and historical medical data. Recently, I suffered from COVID-19, and I went into self-isolation as required by law. I became seriously ill. During my period of quarantine, I was extremely fatigued, breathless and unable to eat anything alone and I was lonely. Friends and family were calling me and interceded on my behalf.

Indeed, the 'foolishness' of God was wiser than men and the weakness of God was stronger than men.

A local GP colleague advised me to monitor my oxygen saturation (SATS) and contact emergency services if they fell below 92. I went through a particularly difficult 3 nights. At one time my

SATS went below 92 at rest. All I could do was rely upon the mercy and grace of God. I slept that third night praying and trusting the Lord to help me for I realised that nothing was going to be of help to me, except God's power. I felt the love and grace of God for even though I was on my own, my loneliness and fear disappeared. I remembered every promise in the word of God and I claimed it in prayer. I declared healing over my body and recovery from the dreadful illness. The following morning, I woke up and felt like a weight had been lifted off my shoulders. I checked my SATS, and I saw that they had improved. I had done nothing except trusting in the Lord. So, putting my trust in the Lord and resting my hope only in Him who sits on the throne is what I understand by "do not lean on your understanding".

> ◉
>
> I rest in his promises for He is faithful.

Medical and scientific advice was indicating that life was slowly coming to a halt but faith in God was reviving the hope that it was going "to be well". Dr H. Saziya trusted in the Lord throughout the night and the Lord helped her to recover. She ceased to lean on her own understanding although she continued to follow the medical advice but she took a much-advanced step of faith and trusted in the Lord who is the author of life. The 'foolishness' of prayer without medication helped her throughout the night when her SATS were falling down. In the midst of her pain, she remembered Isaiah 26:3-4, *"You keep him in perfect peace whose mind is stayed on you, because he trusts in you. Trust in the LORD forever, for the LORD GOD is an everlasting rock".*

All the aforesaid three people agreed that trusting in the Lord is the only better option in life for a better living. Circumstances at the time may dictate otherwise but if one manages to harness and salvage the situation and trust in the Lord against all odds, the benefits for trusting in the Lord are awesome.

It has never been in vain to trust in the Lord.

Psalms 20:6-8 says, *"Now know I that the LORD saves his anointed; he will hear him from his holy heaven with the saving strength of his right hand. Some trust in chariots, and some in horses: but we will remember the name of the LORD our God. They are brought down and fallen, but we are risen, and stand upright.*

Trusting in the Lord is a basic Christian principle of responding to God.

The Psalmists had learned great lessons on trusting in the Lord. He had learned that the Lord will never forsake His anointed ones when they cry unto Him for help. While some would trust in their horses and chariots, the Psalmists had seen that the Lord will never let down those who also trust in Him. Due to His faithfulness in vindicating his anointed ones, the Lord deserved to be trusted for He earned it by His righteous acts.

CHAPTER 5: THE BASIS OF TRUST

We are trusted because of our track record of doing things the right way. We are trusted, if what we say matches with what we do in life. All the people that can be relied upon are people that can be trusted also. So, in a nutshell, the basis of trust is basically what we do to earn the respect that we deserve.

If we are to trust in the Lord with all our hearts, we need to understand the basis upon which we are to trust Him. We need to have solid reasons why we should trust the Lord. We need to investigate the scriptures to find out what God did to all the people that trusted Him.

Trust is not a cheap commodity

It is not a cheap commodity that one can easily find displayed in the marketplace. It does not come so cheap to anyone as if it's a gift by someone trying to throw some favour at you. Trust neither comes on discount nor as

Trust is hard-earned, and trust is deserved.

'buy one get one free'. Trust is not something that one can find at an auction floor and bid for whatever price. Trust has a high price tag in life. Trust is a by-product of sweat; it's a precious reward for having done something worthy of recognition. There is always a reason or validity for trusting anyone. Trust is something that you are given by people for having done something. Trust is like a qualification that one works for and achieve. It's hard-earned, and it's deserved.

Trust is a value you get from people in exchange for the good that you will have done.

The Bible is enriched with stories of what God did for His people so that they can trust Him. First, Adam trusted God for having created everything on earth and put it in his care. Later, God made him a wife to drive out his loneliness and be a life companion. Adam's excitement with what God had done for him is well expressed in Genesis 2:23 when he exclaimed on waking up, *"...This at last is bone of my bones and flesh of my flesh; she shall be called Woman, because she was taken out of (me) Man"*.

God earned the trust by providing them with all that they needed for a living, and He deserved their trust.

Finally, the couple were placed in an orchard called the garden of Eden where every tree with good fruits was given to them to enjoy and the garden had good water reticulation for it had four major rivers with fresh water. Adam and Eve had no good reason not to trust in the Lord when the Lord had given them everything to make them happy in life.

Trust is different from grace from a biblical standpoint. Grace is the undeserved or unmerited favour of God. Grace can also be defined as getting something special from God, out of His divine love, what you don't deserve because of your deeds. In John 3:16 the bible says, *"For God so loved the world, that he gave his only begotten Son, that whosoever believes in him should not perish, but have everlasting life. For God sent not his Son into the world to condemn the world; but that the world through him might be saved. He that believes on him is not condemned: but he that believes not is condemned already, because he has not believed in the name of the only begotten Son of God".*

By our deeds, we did not deserve God's gracious gift of His Son. Isaiah 64:6 (ESV) says, *"We have all become like one who is unclean, and all our righteous deeds are like a polluted garment".* But God by His grace gave us what we did not deserve. He gave us His dear Son while we were yet sinners. Because He can overlook our misdeeds and give us the best in life, He deserves to be trusted.

There was absolutely nothing that the world had done to warrant the enormous love of God. The world in the biblical sense refers to people. People through the ancestry of Adam and Eve, the first people to be created by God, sinned before God by disobeying His word to never eat fruit from the forbidden tree in the midst of the garden. The consequences of disobedience were death to the mortal body and eternal separation of the spirit from fellowshipping with God to a place of eternal punishment. Without having done anything to appease God and pacify His anger, we see God, out of His sheer love, sending His only dear Son, Jesus Christ to the world as a gift of eternal life that whosoever believes in Him should not eternally die and be separated from God but should have eternal life. People did not deserve eternal life, but they can now have eternal life through faith in Jesus Christ. This is grace – undeserved and unmerited favour of God.

Hence, the salvation of people was made free.

Ephesians 2:8-9 says, *"For by grace are you saved through faith; and that not of yourselves: it is the gift of God: Not of works, lest any man should boast".*

It is very clear from the above scripture that salvation is by grace through faith and not of works but by the gift of God. However, Romans 6:23 says, *"For the wages of sin is death; but the gift of God is eternal life through Jesus Christ our Lord"*.

> Death is something we deserve because of sin but God chose to save us through faith in His dear Son Jesus Christ.

In a nutshell, God deserves to be trusted because of the love He has given us. Just for His grace which is unmerited, He deserves our trust. In His mercy, He has not treated us in a manner that we deserve, which is death, but He has shown us, love, by giving us eternal life through Jesus Christ. Instead of a punishment that we deserve, He gives us a gift of eternal life. For that reason alone, God has earned for Himself among us a trust inexplicable. For what the Lord has done for us and what He continues to do for us, He deserves our trust; He earned it.

> The basis of trust is that it is earned and deserved.

Trust is like a reputation. It takes time to build. It is said that it takes a decade to build a reputation, but it only takes a minute to destroy the hard-earned reputation. Trust is likened to a salary, a wage or any remuneration for work that has been done. It does not come cheap; it's hard-earned. One must do something to earn the trust. God in all generations has proven himself trustworthy by the mighty acts He has performed among His people. People trust Him for what He can do.

The criteria of trust

As I was growing up, I came to realise that something can only be trusted if:

- It meets certain basic requirements to be relied upon or to be depended upon.

- It has the strength or capacity to fulfil what it is meant to do or fulfil.

- It has significant positive reviews from people who previously used it or had access to it.

- It has prospective promises about the future.

- It can attract people because of its quality, durability and track record.

These criteria serve as part of the basis of trust. Therefore, if anyone or something is to be trusted, there must be sufficient evidence of its track record, successes, achievements, improvements, developments, and many other things. There must be testimonials or references attached to that person or thing. We often ask ourselves, "Are there other people who can trust you or something? What do they say of you or about the thing? How far can you or that thing be relied upon? How truthful are you or how genuine is the thing?" There must be answers in the affirmative to all these questions before people can make personal commitments to trust in a person or thing.

The bible has a track record of God's dealings with mankind across different generations. Hebrews 11 gives us a list of heroes of faith who through faith in God did extraordinary things or God did extraordinary things through them. By what He did for these people, God earned for Himself trust. It is what you do that earns you the trust.

New employment

In the secular world, if one is to be recruited for a new job or post, the prospective new employer will always ask for references either from previous employment and/or from personal friends. The previous employer is asked by the prospective new employer to give a confidential employment reference detailing the competence for the job applied for as well as the analysis of the applicant's character in terms of commitment, punctuality, skills, availability, absenteeism and the relationship with colleagues. In other words, the prospective employer will be asking for how much one can be trusted. In some instances, a friend or colleague will be asked also to give an opinion about the personal character of the applicant. A friend or work colleague will have to vouch that one has a reliable character, and is   dependable, committed, and employable.

All that I have said so far is figuratively an acid/litmus test (definitive test) for TRUST. The Lord God, the most Supreme Being deserves to be trusted because of the mighty acts that He has done among His people. His attributes and his character attests that He can be trusted. The Bible is the reference book for His mighty acts of God so that He can be trusted by His creation.

CHAPTER 6: TRUST TAKES TIME TO BUILD

Trust takes time to build. Trust is a portrayal of a lifestyle that can be trusted by employers, workmates, and people around you. Trust is a personality that is sweet and inspiring among friends so much that they can find you dependable, honest, credible,

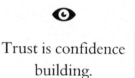

Trust is confidence building.

and trustworthy. There must be sufficient time to build confidence in people to be trusted. This takes time to build in life.

This is the reason why I am saying that TRUST is hard-earned; it's not an easy cheap commodity. It is not something that can be built overnight. There is a proverbial saying that says, *"Rome was never built in a day"* and this is the same with TRUST.

Two people in courtship need time to know each other so well before they can trust each other. Newlyweds need time to stay together and do things together and know each other well before they can both trust each other and have long term goals.

The Merriam-Webster dictionary defines TRUST as:

- Assured reliance on the character, ability, strength or truth of someone or something.

- One in which confidence is placed.

- Dependence on something.

Throughout all generations, the LORD, the Most Supreme Being, the God of gods, and the Lord of lords passed the test of time. He has been among His people doing mighty acts which those who are not His, can testify that He is mighty among His people, and no one can stand against the Holy One of Israel. The Lord God built for Himself a good reputation to be trusted over a very long period. What the Lord God did for Adam, Enoch, Noah, Abraham, Isaac, Jacob, Joseph, David, and Solomon etc, earned Him trust from them. The Psalmist echoed the same sentiments in Psalms 90:1-2, *"LORD, you have been our dwelling place in all generations. Before the mountains were brought forth, or ever you had formed the earth and the world, even from everlasting to everlasting, you are God"*. Based on His faithfulness to His people, the psalmist has every reason to call unto God and declare His omnipresence to His people.

Trust is something that has been tried, tested, and proven

The Collegiate definition of TRUST is "assured reliance on the character, ability, strength or truth of someone or something". Hence, TRUST is something that is tried, tested, and proven to be true to what it should be. The Lord God, the Most Supreme Being, the great I AM, the God of gods and the Lord of lords, proved Himself throughout scriptures that He can be relied upon because He has been tried, tested, and proven throughout generations.

Deuteronomy 10:21 says, *"He is your praise, and He is your God, who has done for you these great and awesome things, which your eyes have seen"*.

There is always something that the Lord has done that demands that we trust in Him. The bible in Proverbs 3:5-6 says,

"Trust in the LORD with all your heart, and do not lean on your own understanding. In all your ways acknowledge him, and he will make straight your paths". There must be very good reasons why King Solomon who is the author of the chapter of the book of Proverbs encouraged his son to "trust in the Lord" with all his heart. He must have tried, tested, and proved this God in his life for him to instruct his dear son likewise.

In Psalm 37:25-26 we hear the Psalmist say, *"I have been young, and now am old, yet I have not seen the righteous forsaken or his children begging for bread. He is ever lending generously, and his children become a blessing"*. The Psalmist is providing proof that for a long time God built for Himself trust by providing for the needs of His righteous people who trust in Him. The Lord earns for Himself trust among the righteous faithful.

The Lord provides bountifully to His righteous people such that they can lend unto others generously and even the children of the righteous become a blessing to others too.

As I pondered on the reasons why King Solomon had to give such an instruction to his dear son, I then realised that he was thinking in terms of the **"9Ps" for Trusting in the Lord** namely:

- Purpose
- Promises
- Provision
- Protection
- Preservation
- Power

- Pathways
- Punishment and
- Promotion

The Lord God worked Himself through all these "**9Ps**" and He proved Himself a reliable and well trusted God to His people. The creator of heaven and earth; the giver of life; the one who has the whole earth in his hands, one who neither sleeps nor slumber and has a good track record of successes, achievements, strength, and power to build or destroy. He deserves to be trusted due to his track record as stated in:

> *Psalms 121:1-8 "I will lift up my eyes unto the hills, from which comes my help. My help comes from the LORD, who made heaven and earth. He will not allow your foot to be moved: he that keeps you will not slumber. Behold, he that keeps Israel shall neither slumber nor sleep. The LORD is your keeper: the LORD is your shade upon your right hand. The sun shall not strike you by day, nor the moon by night. The LORD shall preserve you from all evil: he shall preserve your soul. The LORD shall preserve your going out and your coming in from this time forth, and even forevermore".*

The basis of trusting anybody, let alone the Lord is looking closely on:

- ❖ The Character – honesty, steadfastness, transparency, dependability
- ❖ The Track Record – Accomplishments, strengths and
- ❖ The Vision

I will use this as a plumb line in trying to ascertain the reasons for trusting in the Lord.

God's Character

The Character of God, His unchanging nature and His unfailing love forms the basis on which we build our trust in the Lord. His constant track record of faithfulness, strengths, guidance, protection, provisions and promises accords Him our highest privilege of trust. God's vision for our lives is very clear and He declared that He has better plans for us that will give us a future and hope. These form the basis of our trust in the Lord. All these things I have said so far have taken God a long time to be trusted by His people.

CHAPTER 7: THE PURPOSE FOR THE LORD'S EXISTENCE

The Lord is self-existent. He exists primarily so that we may have our existence in Him since we are His creation. Our purpose is defined in Him. He knows fully well why every one of us was created. Revelation 4:11 says *"Worthy are you, our Lord and God, to receive glory and honour and power, for you created all things, and by your will they existed and were created."* The King James version of the bible would end up saying, *"...and for thy pleasure they are and were created"*. The Lord ought to be trusted for to Him belongs our purpose which we must live to fulfil.

King Solomon had to encourage his son to trust in the Lord with all his heart because he realised that we should live to fulfil the lord's plans and purpose in our lives.

We should never lean on our understanding but on the plans and purposes of the Lord.

My heart was intrigued when I read the writings of William Wilberforce, David Livingstone, Martin Luther King Jr, and the wonderful Bible. The more I read about these writings, the more I began to realise that God in every generation, raises men and women to accomplish His divine plan and purposes on earth. These men and women stood against the odds of their times and fought against the evil of their times without fear, simply because they had realised that God had a special plan and purpose for their lives.

William Wilberforce was a British politician, philanthropist, and leader of the movement to abolish the slave trade. He was a native of Kingston upon Hull, Yorkshire, United Kingdom. He began his political career in 1780, eventually becoming an independent Member of Parliament for Yorkshire. He died on 29 July 1833.

David Livingstone was a Scottish missionary, doctor, abolitionist, and explorer who lived in the 1800s. He sought to bring Christianity, commerce, and "civilization" to Africa and undertook three extensive expeditions throughout much of the continent of Africa. He died on 1 May 1873.

Martin Luther King, Jr., was an African American Baptist minister and social rights activist in the United States in the 1950s and '60s. He was a leader of the American civil rights movement. He organized several peaceful protests as head of the Southern Christian Leadership Conference, including the March on Washington in 1963. He fought for the freedom of the African American people. He was assassinated on 4 April 1968.

These great men in history when they sought the Lord, He revealed to each one of them His divine plans over their lives. When they pursued those plans and purposes, they had every good reason for living and that is what made each of them great in their respective generations.

They were trusted by the people because they lived purpose driven lives.

Although history can now recognise their work and reward them for doing great things for humanity, it was not so during their times. A man's work is often not appreciated while he still lives but when he dies people will begin to realise his work and begin to give credit to it.

I often ask myself, "What were these men's motivations? What gave them the impetus to stand alone for the values they believed? Why didn't they give up?" When I read the writings of these men, I then realised that they were consumed by the zeal of their convictions and belief. They understood that God was raising them to do something in their time to fulfil God's divine plan and purposes.

> They defined themselves in the plan and purposes of God.

William Wilberforce, a British politician, philanthropist, and a leader of the movement to abolish the African slave trade in the 18th & 19th century once said, "It is the true duty of every man to promote the happiness of his fellow-creatures to the utmost of his power". These words were reinforced in his belief by John Newton who wrote him a letter when he was about to give up and said, "God has raised you up for the good of the church and the good of the nation, maintain your friendship with Pitt (a former British Prime Minister), continue in Parliament, who knows that but for such a time as this God has brought you into public life and has a purpose for you".

Indeed, God had a divine purpose for the man called William Wilberforce. History tells us that he fought tooth and nail for the abolishment of the African slave trade. He tabled several bills in United Kingdom Parliament for almost 20 years demanding justice and fair treatment for the black or dark-skinned people who were being captured in Africa and brought to Europe and America in ships to work in plantations and other forms of industry as slaves.

The practice was a great source of revenue on the stock market and yet the slaves were not treated with fairness at the stock market by their slave masters as they were being auctioned and let alone being taken as property.

William Wilberforce was quick to realise in his early 1920s that God created all men equal, and that every man deserves fair and equal treatment as a human being. He saw how evil had degraded men and caused men to suppress and oppress one another. He was quick to realise that God wanted all people to do unto others as they would like them to do unto them and yet, few people realised that. Therefore, in every generation, God raises individuals who will define their purpose of existence by considering God's plan and purposes.

Men like William Wilberforce were raised by God to fight against the injustices of the slave trade and bring them to an end. God raised him because he was such a man who believed that "It is the true duty of every man to promote the happiness of his fellow-creatures to the utmost of his power". He also believed in the words of John Newton who said that "God raised you up for the good of the church and for the good of the nation…and has a purpose for you". With these words and many others, William perceived that he had a duty before God to promote the happiness of his fellow men and not only that because he also fought against animal cruelty. His purpose in life was the emancipation of slaves and fair treatment of animals. Wilberforce was trusted for the purpose of his existence just as God almighty is always trusted for the purpose of His existence.

Having understood this divine concept, King Solomon had to instruct his son in Proverbs 3:5-6 to *"Trust in the LORD with all your heart, and do not lean on your own understanding. In all your ways acknowledge him, and he will make straight your paths."* King

Solomon understood that his father King David trusted in the Lord just as the former patriarchs had trusted in the Lord and God handpicked them in due times to fulfil His divine plan and purposes.

Outside God, there is no purpose for men

I will use the following analogy to illustrate the above point. Each item in a house has its purpose defined by the

So, trusting in the Lord will enable God to raise you in due time to fulfil His divine plan and purpose.

manufacturer. Each homeowner will purchase these items/gadgets as defined by the manufacturer. Certain items/gadgets can be placed in the same room for instance, in the kitchen, but they will be for different purposes. Each item is valuable only if it can serve the interests/purpose of the owner. The moment it fails to serve the purpose for which the owner bought it, it will be thrown away and be recycled.

Jesus in John 15:2 made a very remarkable statement, *"Every branch in me that does not bear fruit he takes away, and every branch that does bear fruit he prunes, that it may bear more fruit".* Bearing fruit is the purpose of every branch. If it fails to fulfil the purpose of the gardener then it's no longer fit to remain attached to the tree and be in the garden. It is just fit to be thrown away. Similarly, our lives outside God's purpose become meaningless.

Ecclesiastes 1:2, *"Vanity of vanities, says the Preacher, vanity of vanities! All is vanity".*

God exists to be trusted by His creation. Creation trusts him for who He is and what He does. Purpose is the reason for existence. It is the function of a thing that defines a thing or somebody. In the scriptures, God is known by various names by which His purpose in human life is expressed. Whenever those who trusted in the Lord were in crisis and they turned unto Him; we find God revealing his purpose of existence by giving them what they needed to make them happy. Mankind then would give God names in relation to what he would have done to them which would be the cause for trusting Him. Below are a few examples of such names.

He is:

- **Jehovah-Jireh** meaning the Lord who provides [Genesis 22:14]. At Mt Moriah, God had provided a lamb of sacrifice to Abraham in substitution of Isaac his son whom He had asked to be offered as a sacrifice in a test of his obedience. Abraham attested that God could provide something, where nothing is available in the first place.

- **Jehovah-Tsidkenu** meaning the Lord our righteousness [Jeremiah 23:6]. God promised Israel that He was going to give them a king who was going to be caring as a Shepherd and would govern them in righteousness. They were going to call him "the Lord our righteousness" because of what he was going to do. This meant that God was going to be trusted for His righteousness by His people. Righteousness means right dealings with His people. God was going to provide Israel with a right king who would deal righteously with His people. So, He deserved to be trusted.

- **Jehovah-Nissi** meaning the Lord our banner [Exodus 17:15]. God gave victory to Israel over the battle against the Amalekites through the intercession that Moses as their leader made in the mountain with Aaron and Hur lifting his hands. The Lord is the one who can be trusted to give his people victory over their enemies. The Lord deserves to be trusted because He can give victory.

- **Jehovah-M'Kaddesh** meaning **Jehovah** who Sanctifies [Leviticus 20:7-8]. To sanctify is to set apart for a holy purpose. It is God who can set apart His people for a holy purpose. In all generations, God set apart his people for a holy purpose. He deserves to be trusted by His people.

- **Jehovah-Shammah** meaning the Lord is there [Ezekiel 48:35]. God promised His people that He would dwell with them in the new city and the name of the city would be Jehovah-Shammah. Even in the new earth [Revelation 21:3] God promised to dwell among His people and be their God. To be their God means to be on the side of His people to protect, provide, preserve, and purify them for as long as He is among them. The Lord is to be trusted for His ever-presence among His people.

- **Jehovah-Shalom** meaning the Lord is our peace [Judges 6:24]. It came a time in Israel that the Midianites for seven years waited for Israel to sow their crops and when it's about time to harvest they would come and fight them and loot everything including their livestock. When Israel then cried unto the Lord God, the Lord sent an angel to Gideon to appoint him as a leader who would deliver Israel from the Midianites. Through Gideon, the Lord was bringing back peace to Israel so that she may rest. Gideon wanted assurance that God was indeed going to use him to deliver Israel from the Midianites and restore peace in the land. So, he asked if he could go home from the threshing floor and bring some presents to the angel. The angel asked him to lay the presents on the rock and the angel touched the presents with the staff that Gideon had and the offerings on the altar were consumed with fire. Gideon called the place Jehovah Shalom meaning the Lord is our peace. Gideon led the army and won the victory and restored the peace. It was the Lord God who brought victory to Israel and restored peace. Indeed, the Lord God deserves to be trusted for giving victory over our enemies and for restoring peace. The Lord God exists to give us victories and peace that surpasses understanding [Philippians 4:7].

- **Jehovah-Raah** meaning the Lord is our shepherd [Ezekiel 34:11-16; Psalms 23:1]. A shepherd guides and protects the sheep as well as lead them to green pastures and still waters. The Lord God promised Israel when her children were all scattered because of the negligence of the leaders that He was to gather them Himself as a shepherd and bring them together and shepherd them. So, the Lord God exists to shepherd His people. He is Jehovah-Raah.

- **Jehovah-Rapha** meaning the Lord that heals [Exodus 15:26]. The Lord God promised the nation of Israel that no plagues or diseases such as those that had hit the Egyptians were going to hit them if they took heed of His statutes for, He was going to heal them of all their diseases. He called Himself Jehovah Rapha meaning the Lord that heals you. He exists to be the healer among His people.

- **Jehovah-Sabaoth** meaning the Lord of Hosts [1Samuel 17:45; Joshua 5:14-15]. The Lord God comes to lead the armies of His people to victory as Captain of the Armies of God in heaven and on earth. He exists to fight for His people and to give them victories. He declares that the battles for His people are His battles. Those who have trusted him for victory He gave them victories. Indeed, the Lord God deserves to be trusted.

God exists to be the source and reason of existence. God defines a thing, and He gives it its purpose as it finds the purpose in Him and as expressed in Him. Therefore, God exists to be trusted by His creation for everything that the creation should do.

People were created in the image and likeness of God to accomplish His divine purposes. The purposes of man are defined in God. Outside of God, life is meaningless and without purpose. This is the reason why man goes back to the creator to consult on what needs to be done because the purpose is well defined in God.

Through the names of God, we learn that God is looking for people who can trust Him as depicted by His names so that He can find people to pick and use for His divine plan and purpose. King Solomon wanted his son to qualify before God for such a choice in due time.

For our physiological needs, we find our provisions in the Lord. Unless He provides us with water, air, food, health, and many other essentials of life, we find ourselves without any other alternative source to our provisions. Unless the Lord provides peace and safety, we struggle but in vain to achieve them on our own.

Psalms 127:1 *"Unless the LORD builds the house, those who build it labour in vain. Unless the LORD watches over the city, the watchman stays awake in vain".*

God exists to give us all that we need for life and for that purpose, we have every reason to encourage each other to trust in the Lord.

This concept is what the American Psychologist Abraham H. Maslow tried to explain in his thesis on the Hierarchy of Human Needs when he stated his five levels that need to be satisfied before one can reach the self-actualization moment in life which can also be called the "Aha! moments". I will refer and explain in detail what he states as I correlate each level with how it fits in the teaching of trusting in God for everything in life.

The author of the book of the gospel of John in the Bible tried to convey the same concept or belief that everything exists because of the Lord God and without Him nothing can exist and find meaning.

John 1:1-3 *In the beginning was the Word, and the Word was with God, and the Word was God. The same was in the beginning with God. All things were made by him; and without him was not anything made that was made.*

Life has meaning only if it can be defined under the divine perspective. This explains why King Solomon had to instruct his son to TRUST in the Lord and never to lean on his own understanding. King Solomon in his writings in the book of Ecclesiastes looking from a divine perspective declared that it is "vanity of vanities; all is vanity" - Ecclesiastes 1:2.

Ecclesiastes 1:14 *I have seen all the works that are done under the sun; and behold, all is vanity and like grasping the wind.*

Indeed, the Lord God exists to give true meaning and purpose to His creation. Without waiting upon the LORD and TRUSTING the LORD, everything that is done under the sun is just a chasing of the wind and it's all vanity.

I will add to this section of the first "P" by saying that the purpose of God's existence is to give us a purpose in life or meaning to life. William Wilberforce understood this and said, "God Almighty has set before me two Great Objects: the suppression of the Slave Trade and the Reformation of Manners". God raised him just to fulfil what was conceived in his heart.

Allow me to share my testimony on this subject. I was born of devout Christian parents who taught us as children to pray, read the bible and fear the Lord. I grew up to love the Lord so much at a very tender age. I lived a different life as a young kid being obedient to my parents and loving my church. One day while I was below the age of ten, whether I was in this body or not I don't know but I was caught up into heaven just like what happened to the Apostle Paul. I saw a city whose buildings and furnishings are incomparable to anything on earth. Until this day, I have not yet found anything as beautiful as things I saw in a vision. The end of the vision was that all people in heaven were called at a certain time to come before the throne for service. None of the people I saw, ever stood to the height of the ankle of the one who was seated on the throne as they came to take their positions. People were of different nationalities and languages but when He spoke to all, He spoke in one language, and everyone heard and understood in his own language. We were all given tasks to go and do in the fields to which we were allocated. Going to do your tasks was what was called "service". The word "service" carries a different connotation to us today. In that vision, I was assigned to my field to go and do service.

Service to us is going to attend church while in heaven it is doing what you have been assigned to do.

Little did I know then as a young kid that God had called me to be a minister of the gospel. From that moment, God raised me and preserved me so that I may be a light in a dark world. God exists to reveal His divine plan and purpose over my life. While still at a tender age, I saw myself preaching in English but to multitudes in Europe and at that time I knew nothing of geography. I did not know that God was raising me and preparing me to bring reverse missiology to Europe from Africa. As I write this book, I am the founding and Senior Pastor of Harvest of Souls Ministries UK which is based in the United Kingdom. God exists to define my purpose for living. My life outside God's purpose is worthless and without meaning.

Life is fulfilling when you live to fulfil your God-given purpose.

Friend, if you trust in the Lord with all your heart you will find out that God will define the purpose for your life. At the end of our journeys of life, we shall all be rewarded for having fulfilled our purposes on earth. If we lived for ourselves, surely, we would not expect to be rewarded for the things that benefited ourselves. A person is only rewarded for those things which you will have done for others.

William Wilberforce, David Livingstone, Martin Luther King Jr and many others found the fulfilment of life when they lived to fulfil God's plan and purpose for their lives. You can too, if only you learn to trust in the Lord with all your heart and never to lean on your understanding and in all your ways to consider Him.

Allow me to end this chapter by stating categorically that THE PURPOSE FOR A THING IS THE REASON FOR ITS EXISTENCE. Anything continues to live or exist in order to achieve/accomplish/fulfil/attain to its intended purposes. Once anything can no longer function according to its intended purposes, it is no longer fit to continue to exist but to be discarded, side-lined, obliterated or thrown away.

For this reason, God exists to sustain everything by His own power and authority. He exists to give meaning to his creation. He is the life for every creation. Everything depends on Him for life and continued existence. God earned who He is by His very divine nature and deserves to be trusted for what He is able to do for His creation. He earned it and He deserve it and to Him be all glory. It Pays to Trust God. This is a simple Principle of Responding to God. Let's do what we have been created to do just as He exists to do what He exists for.

Amen.

SECTION 2: TRUST IS DESERVED

CHAPTER 8: THE PROMISES OF THE LORD

The Lord God is a promise-keeping God. 2 Corinthians 1:20 (ESV) says, *"For all the promises of God find their Yes in him (Jesus Christ). That is why it is through him that we utter our Amen to God for his glory"*. Since all the promises of God are yes and amen in Christ Jesus, the Lord deserves to be trusted as a promise keeper.

> 👁
>
> He who has something has the power to promise something to the one who does not have on his terms and conditions.

Psalms 24:1, A Psalm of David says, *"The earth is Jehovah's, and the fullness thereof; the world, and they that dwell therein"*. This means that God owns everything on earth, and He can promise to give anything on earth to anyone whom He is pleased with. A promise can similarly be viewed as a reward for fulfilling certain terms and conditions.

The Webster-Merriam dictionary defines "Promise" as:

> 👁
>
> If anyone can fulfil his promises, it means that person deserves to be trusted and relied upon.

i.   a declaration that one will do or refrain from doing something specified or

ii.   a legally binding declaration that gives the person to whom it is made a right to expect or claim the performance or forbearance of a specified act or the reason to expect something.

iii.   [as an intransitive verb] "to give ground for expectation".

The Bible which is God's word to his people contains declarations of what He is able to do for His people if only they are willing to obey Him and love Him as their God. The Bible shows how God legally binds Himself to His word to fulfil it to his people. For that reason, He deserves to be trusted.

Deuteronomy 28:1-2 (ESV) clearly sets the terms and conditions for receiving blessings/curses from God.

> *"And if you faithfully obey the voice of the LORD your God, being careful to do all his commandments that I command you today, the LORD your God will set you high above all the nations of the earth. And all these blessings shall come upon you and overtake you, if you obey the voice of the LORD your God".*

Deuteronomy 28:1-14 gives declarations of blessings which I term "promises" and verses 15-68 gives a list of curses which I term judgements/punishments for disobedience. I will reiterate that he who has something to give will always set out his own terms and conditions under which he/she makes available that which can be given. God has the possessor of everything on earth has the prerogative to set His own terms and conditions.

One quick example I could single out if His people chose to disobey His commands is Deuteronomy 28:30-33, *"You shall betroth a wife, but another man shall ravish her. You shall build a house, but you shall not dwell in it. You shall plant a vineyard, but you shall not enjoy its fruit. Your ox shall be slaughtered before your eyes, but you shall not eat any of it. Your donkey shall be seized before your face but shall not be restored to you. Your sheep shall be given to your enemies, but there shall be no one to help you. Your sons and your daughters shall be given to another people, while your eyes look on and fail with longing for them all day long, but you shall be helpless. A nation that you have not known shall eat up the fruit of your ground and of all your labours, and you shall be only oppressed and crushed continually".*

I can safely compare its fulfilment of the promise with Judges 6:1-10, *"The people of Israel did what was evil in the sight of the LORD, and the LORD gave them into the hand of Midian seven years. And the hand of Midian overpowered Israel, and because of Midian, the people of Israel made for themselves the dens that are in the mountains and the caves and the strongholds. For whenever the Israelites planted crops, the Midianites and the Amalekites and the people of the East would come up against them. They would encamp against them and devour the produce of the land, as far as Gaza, and leave no sustenance in Israel and no sheep or ox or donkey. For they would come up with their livestock and their tents; they would come like locusts in number—both they and their camels could not be counted—so that they laid waste the land as they came in. And Israel was brought very low because of Midian. And the people of Israel cried out for help to the LORD.*

When the people of Israel cried out to the LORD on account of the Midianites, the LORD sent a prophet to the people of Israel. And he said to them, "Thus says the LORD, the God of Israel: I led you up from Egypt and brought you out of the house of slavery. And I delivered you from the hand of the Egyptians and from the hand of all who oppressed you and drove them out before you and gave you, their land. And I said to you, 'I am the LORD your God; you shall not fear the gods of the Amorites in whose land you dwell.' But you have not obeyed my voice."

> He was reminding his son that God is a promise keeper.

Understanding these events, King Solomon was also quick to advise his son in Proverbs 3:5-6 that he should trust in the Lord so he may learn to obey His word so that none of the curses of Deuteronomy should ever come his way as they did in the times of the Judges.

A Promise Keeper

When people began to increase in number on earth, the Bible says in Genesis 6:5-8, *"The LORD saw that the wickedness of man was great in the earth, and that every intention of the thoughts of his heart was only evil continually. And the LORD regretted that he had made man on the earth, and it grieved him to his heart. So, the LORD said, "I will blot out man whom I have created from the face of the land, man and animals and creeping things and birds of the heavens, for I am sorry that I have made them." But Noah found favour in the eyes of the LORD".*

God was disgusted by the wickedness that was prevalent on earth. He came to Noah; the only righteous man and told him of his intentions towards the entire earth. As an act of his grace and a reward to Noah for his righteousness, God gave a promise to Noah.

"For behold, I will bring a flood of waters upon the earth to destroy all flesh in which is the breath of life under heaven. Everything that is on the earth shall die. But I will establish my covenant with you, and you shall come into the ark, you, your sons, your wife, and your sons' wives with you" – Genesis 6:17-18.

God promised to destroy all flesh on earth with a flood. His second promise was to establish a covenant with Noah and his family that he would not destroy them together with all flesh but would save them with an ark. Noah needed to trust in the Lord that what He had said was surely going to pass.

The Bible says that Noah and his family believed God and they went ahead to build an ark even when it was difficult to believe such an event because there hadn't been any rains since the creation of the earth. When they had completed the task in faith, God was well pleased with Noah and his family, and He was ready to fulfil His promise. God is a promise keeper, and He deserves to be trusted.

Genesis 7:1, *"Then the LORD said to Noah, "Go into the ark, you and all your household, for I have seen that you are righteous before me in this generation".*

Genesis 7:4 *"For in seven days I will send rain on the earth forty days and forty nights, and every living thing that I have made I will blot out from the face of the ground."*

Genesis 7:6-7 *"Noah was six hundred years old when the flood of waters came upon the earth. And Noah and his sons and his wife and his sons' wives with him went into the ark to escape the waters of the flood".*

Genesis 7:10 *"And after seven days the waters of the flood came upon the earth".*

Surely, God deserves to be trusted because He keeps his word/promise. In the case of Noah, he destroyed the entire flesh except what he wanted to preserve. At his appointed time, the floodwaters came upon the earth. Everything happened just as God had said it.

We have a natural tendency to trust anyone who keeps a promise. God keeps promises. Therefore, He should be trusted.

God watches over His word

Isaiah 55:10-13 says, "For as the rain comes down, and the snow from heaven, and returns not there, but waters the earth, and makes it bring forth and bud, that it may give seed to the sower, and bread to the eater: So shall my word be that goes forth out of my mouth: it shall not return unto me void, but it shall accomplish that which I please, and it shall prosper in the thing for which I sent it. For you shall go out with joy and be led forth with peace: the mountains and the hills shall break forth before you into singing, and all the trees of the field shall clap their hands. Instead of the thorn shall come up the cypress tree, and instead of the brier shall come up the myrtle tree: and it shall be to the LORD for a name, for an everlasting sign that shall not be cut off".

The prophet Isaiah in the preceding passage is very clear that God is faithful to his word and his promises. He ordained that there be rain and snow on earth for the benefit of all living creatures and since then, He has not relented on his promises. God's word and promises are intended to accomplish His purposes throughout all generations. God is a promise keeper and for this reason alone, He deserves to be trusted.

Another incident is in the account of Jeremiah 25:11-12 where God through the mouth of Jeremiah promised the nation of Israel that they were to go into exile for seventy years because Nebuchadnezzar, king of Babylon was going to besiege their land and take them captive. After the set time, God was going to avenge for His people. This happened just as God had promised when you read the full account. God is a promise keeper, and He deserves to be trusted.

If you do your part, God will do His part:

Moses a great leader of the nation of Israel when they made an exodus from Egypt, gathered the nation to give them a catalogue of God's promises for as long as they were able to listen and obey God's commandments.

Deuteronomy 7:12 says, *"If you pay attention to these laws and are careful to follow them, then the LORD your God will keep his covenant of love with you, as he swore to your ancestors. 13 He will love you and bless you and increase your numbers. He will bless the fruit of your womb, the crops of your land—your grain, new wine, and olive oil—the calves of your herds and the lambs of your flocks in the land he swore to your ancestors to give you. 14 You will be blessed more than any other people; none of your men or women will be childless, nor will any of your livestock be without young. 15 The LORD will keep you free from every disease. He will not inflict on you the horrible diseases you knew in Egypt, but he will inflict them on all who hate you".*

The passage of scripture above is packed with wonderful promises of success or declarations of God to his people namely:

- *The LORD your God will keep his covenant of love with you*

- *He will love you and bless you and increase your numbers*

- *He will bless the fruit of your womb and the crops of your land*

- *You will be blessed more than any other people*

- *None of your men or women will be childless*

- *The LORD will keep you free from every disease*

Moses' word to the nation of Israel was simple: If you do your part, God will do His part. Their part was to pay attention to God's laws and to carefully follow them. This would put God under divine, legal and binding obligation to fulfil what He promised. In other words, every promise has a condition attached to it. A promise is like a contract; it has terms and conditions to bind the parties to the contract.

God kept his word to Abraham

Genesis 17:1-2, *"When Abram was ninety-nine years old the LORD appeared to Abram and said to him, "I am God Almighty; walk before me, and be blameless, that I may make my covenant between me and you and may multiply you greatly."*

Genesis 17:7-8, *"And I will establish my covenant between me and you and your offspring after you throughout their generations for an everlasting covenant, to be God to you and to your offspring after you. And I will give to you and to your offspring after you the land of your sojourning, all the land of Canaan, for an everlasting possession, and I will be their God."*

He keeps His covenant to the third and fourth generations.

Indeed, God is a covenant-keeping God. What God promised to Father Abraham that is what He keeps on doing to His generations up to this very day. Time and again in the bible, we have seen God punishing the nation of Israel for breaking the terms of his promises, but He has never disowned them as a nation and as His people. God acts as a father to the nation of Israel. A father hates the mistakes of the children and disciplines them for their mistakes, but he does not disown them. As the prophet Isaiah says, "He knows the better thoughts he has for his people".

Hebrews 12:5 says, *"And have you completely forgotten this word of encouragement that addresses you as a father addresses his son? It says, "My son, do not make light of the Lord's discipline, and do not lose heart when he rebukes you, 6 because the Lord disciplines the one, he loves, and he chastens everyone he accepts as his son." 7 Endure hardship as discipline; God is treating you as his children. For what children are not disciplined by their father? 8 If you are not disciplined—and everyone undergoes discipline— then you are not legitimate, not true sons and daughters at all. 9 Moreover, we have all had human fathers who disciplined us, and we respected them for it. How much more should we submit to the Father of spirits and live! 10 They disciplined us for a little while as they thought best; but God disciplines us for our good, in order that we may share in his holiness. 11 No discipline seems pleasant at the time, but painful. Later, however, it produces a harvest of righteousness and peace for those who have been trained by it".*

Purpose of God's Discipline

God made a covenant with Abraham who was obedient to him. God promised Abraham that He would bless him and all his future descendants. There is no way that God is going to break that covenant because it was sealed in blood [Genesis 15:8-15].

However, God has promised to fulfil with the descendants of Abraham. If the descendants break the terms of the promises, He will punish them [discipline] for breaking the terms

> The purpose of discipline is God's way of finding how to honour his promises while dealing with disobedience.

but He can't fail to honour the covenant with Abraham by disowning his descendants. He disciplines because He still loves His people as descendants of Abraham.

To this day, God has been faithful to his promises to Abraham and the nation of Israel. Nations may try to disperse the nation of Israel, but they have been failing because God is keeping his promises to Abraham and his descendants.

Another promise that God gave to Abraham is in Genesis 12:3:

"I will bless those who bless you, and him who dishonours you I will curse, and in you all the families of the earth shall be blessed."

We have seen the fulfilment of the passage above. Nations like America that support Israel are blessed. Nations that oppose Israel have all sorts of turmoil going on in their countries or regions. So, if God's promises remain true to this day, it follows therefore that He deserves to be trusted.

David's Charge to Solomon

1 Chronicles 28:9, *"And you, Solomon my son, know the God of your father and serve him with a whole heart and with a willing mind, for the LORD searches all hearts and understands every plan and thought. If you seek him, he will be found by you, but if you forsake him, he will cast you off forever".*

David charged his son, heir to the throne that he should trust in the Lord if he does not want to see himself cast off forever. To trust in the Lord meant to *"serve him with a whole heart and with a willing mind".* If he was going to do what his father advised him to do, then God was bound to honour the promises he made to David concerning his throne.

King Solomon as a son who had seen how God was faithful to his father King David was quick to encourage his dear son too, "to trust in the Lord" with all his heart, mind and soul. He saw God keeping his promises to his father David just as He had said to Abraham, Isaac and Jacob, the patriarchs of Israel. He saw how God loved the patriarchs and all other faithful ancestors and how he blessed them for having trusted in Him. He saw how God blessed the fruit of their wombs and the increase of their crops in their lifetime because of trusting in the Lord. Solomon could testify that God kept his promise to keep His people from the diseases which other nations suffered. God is a promise keeper.

King Solomon knew that God had promised his father David that He was going to establish his throne forever and his successor was going to be blessed in every area of life. Indeed, he was a testimony to God's faithfulness to His promises. So, King Solomon thought to break the silence and said to his son, "Trust in the Lord with all your heart" and "lean not on your understanding".

Perhaps, King Solomon was making a recollection of events soon after succeeding his father, King David when he had a dream. 1Kings 3:4 says, *"The king went to Gibeon to offer sacrifices, for that was the most important high place, and Solomon offered a thousand burnt offerings on that altar. 5 At Gibeon the LORD appeared to Solomon during the night in a dream, and God said, "Ask for whatever you want me to give you." 6 Solomon answered, "You have shown great kindness to your servant, my father David, because he was faithful to you and righteous and upright in heart. You have continued this great kindness to him and have given him a son to sit on his throne this very day. 7 "Now, LORD my God, you have made your servant king in place of my father David. But I am only a little child and do not know how to carry out my duties. 8 Your servant is here among the people you have chosen, a great people, too numerous to count or number. 9 So give your servant a discerning heart to govern your people and to distinguish between right and wrong. For who is able to govern this great people of yours?" 10 The Lord was pleased that Solomon had asked for this. 11 So God said to him, "Since you have asked for this and not for long life or wealth for yourself, nor have asked for the death of your enemies but for discernment in administering justice, 12 I will do what you have asked. I will give you a wise and discerning heart, so that there will never have been anyone like you, nor will there ever be. 13 Moreover, I will give you what you have not asked for— both wealth and honour—so that in your lifetime you will have no equal among kings. 14 And if you walk in obedience to me and keep my decrees and commands as David your father did, I will give you a long life." 15 Then Solomon awoke—and he realized it had been a dream".*

Thereafter, King Solomon was faced with a very terrible situation that was to tests his leadership as a wise king. He remembered how he had a wise ruling in the following case:

1Kings 3:16 *Now two prostitutes came to the king and stood before him. 17 One of them said, "Pardon me, my lord. This woman and I live in the same house, and I had a baby while she was there with me. 18 The third day after my child was born, this woman also had a baby. We were alone; there was no one in the house but the two of us. 19 "During the night this woman's son died because she lay on him. 20 So she got up in the middle of the night and took my son from my side while I your servant was asleep. She put him by her breast and put her dead son by my breast. 21 The next morning, I got up to nurse my son—and he was dead! But when I looked at him closely in the morning light, I saw that it wasn't the son I had borne." 22 The other woman said, "No! The living one is my son; the dead one is yours." But the first one insisted, "No! The dead one is yours; the living one is mine." And so, they argued before the king. 23 The king said, "This one says,*

'My son is alive, and your son is dead,' while that one says, 'No! Your son is dead and mine is alive.'" 24 Then the king said, "Bring me a sword." So, they brought a sword for the king. 25 He then gave an order: "Cut the living child in two and give half to one and half to the other." 26 The woman whose son was alive was deeply moved out of love for her son and said to the king, "Please, my lord, give her the living baby! Don't kill him!" But the other said, "Neither I nor you shall have him. Cut him in two!" 27 Then the king gave his ruling: "Give the living baby to the first woman. Do not kill him; she is his mother." 28 When all Israel heard the verdict the king had given, they held the king in awe, because they saw that he had wisdom from God to administer justice".

Leaning on one's understanding was in no way going to have made King Solomon famous as a wise king. King Solomon knew that he gained wisdom by trusting in the Lord and the Lord kept His promises because He is a covenant promise keeper. Therefore, it was quite expedient for him to encourage his son in Proverbs 3:5 to *"trust in the Lord" with all his heart, mind, and soul.*

God keeps his promises to the God-fearing people. The book of Job has a story of a man called Job who feared God and shunned evil and he enjoyed God's blessings as God had promised.

Job 1:1 says, *"In the land of Uz there lived a man whose name was Job. This man was blameless and upright; he feared God and shunned evil. 2 He had seven sons and three daughters, 3 and he owned seven thousand sheep, three thousand camels, five hundred yoke of oxen and five hundred donkeys, and had a large number of servants. He was the greatest man among all the people of the East".*

This account in Job is evidence that God keeps his promises to his people as Moses had said in Deuteronomy 7:12-15 (ESV):

"And because you listen to these rules and keep and do them, the LORD your God will keep with you the covenant and the steadfast love that he swore to your fathers. He will love you, bless you, and multiply you. He will also bless the fruit of your womb and the fruit of your ground, your grain and your wine and your oil, the increase of your herds and the young of your flock, in the land that he swore to your fathers to give you. You shall be blessed above all peoples. There shall not be male or female barren among you or among your livestock. And the LORD will take away from you all sickness, and none of the evil diseases of Egypt, which you knew, will he inflict on you, but he will lay them on all who hate you.

Even though Job had lost everything in life because of the attack that was waged against him by Satan, Job still had "trust in the Lord" and sinned not against God. He feared God and shunned evil. To fear does not carry the meaning of being timid and expecting to be consumed in one's anger but it implies the idea of approaching God with respect, humility, and obedience to whatever He says. Whom you trust, you can always respect and obey. Job respected and humbled himself before God as he obeyed God's word and never allowed any sinful words to proceed out of his mouth against God and God honoured him and blessed him for keeping his commands.

Job 1:22 *"In all this Job sinned not, nor charged God foolishly".*

Job 42:12 *"The LORD blessed the latter part of Job's life more than the former part. He had fourteen thousand sheep, six thousand camels, a thousand yoke of oxen and a thousand donkeys. 13 And he also had seven sons and three daughters. 14*

The first daughter he named Jemimah, the second Keziah and the third Keren-Happuch. 15 Nowhere in all the land were there found women as beautiful as Job's daughters, and their father granted them an inheritance along with their brothers. 16 After this, Job lived a hundred and forty years; he saw his children and their children to the fourth generation. 17 And so Job died, an old man and full of years".

Oh! What a joy? When you see the faithfulness of God in keeping his divine promises to those that fear and trust in Him. God doubled Job's former blessings as a reward for keeping his trust in the Lord amid severe adversity. God can also add beauty as a blessing to those that fear and trust him.

Job 42: 15 says, *"Nowhere in all the land were there found women as beautiful as Job's daughters.*

I can as well cite another example when God kept his promises to Joseph the son of Jacob in Genesis 37. Joseph had two separate dreams in which God promised him greatness. Genesis 41-46 has an account of how God kept his promises to Joseph when he rose to second in command in Egypt from Pharaoh King of Egypt.

My Personal Testimonies

It is quite compelling that I should also give my personal testimony of God's faithfulness in keeping his promises to those who fear and trust in Him.

Early rains in a dry season

My father, the late Nyson Chikonobaya Muzangaza was a God-fearing man who trusted in the Lord for everything. Every day he would wake up about 1am and pray until about 4am. He was a man of prayer. He trusted and believed in God and God revealed great secrets to him.

I remember one day in 1968 when he woke up to tell us that God had told him of a great famine that was going to strike upon Zimbabwe (then Rhodesia). He was advised by God to sow drought-resistant crops like sorghum and finger millet (mapfunde, zviyo, nemhunga in Shona). He was also given an early date of planting of late October to have put all seeds in the ground for rains were going to be scarce and sporadic.

My dad trusted in the word of the Lord. He did his winter ploughing and asked us to sow the seeds by late October in all fields. Only a small portion on an anthill at our request did he plant white maize for our roasting. In that year, our family was the only family in the communal lands of Gweshe, Chiweshe that harvested that season, and many wondered how, but we knew it was the Lord's doing. God keeps his promises to the God-fearing servants and those who trust in him.

My Personal Calling into Ministry

My other personal testimony that God deserves to be trusted for He keeps His promises is like this. Way before I was conceived in my mother's womb, there was a prophetic message that was given to my parents during a prayer service. They were told that one of their sons was going to receive a divine calling of God to enter the ministry of preaching the gospel. They did not know which of the four sons had the calling in a family of six. They educated all of us and made us attain our professional qualifications. It seemed God had not spoken since there was no fulfilment of the prophetic message for quite a long time.

But God is not a man that He should lie and neither the son of man that He should repent. For in Isaiah 55:11 says, *"so shall my word be that goes out from my mouth; it shall not return to me empty, but it shall accomplish that which I purpose, and shall succeed in the thing for which I sent it"*.

In the fullness of God's time against all odds, prophecy was fulfilled. I, Mystery, 2nd of the 4 sons received a divine calling to be a Pastor. I desperately resisted the calling but in vain. I went for training at the Living Waters Theological Seminary and obtained my Diploma in Bible and Theology and later I did my B.A. Degree in Bible/Theology with ICI, Brussels, Belgium.

God is never in a hurry to fulfil His promises because He has eternity in His hands. There is no delay with God because He is the time.

God promised my parents that one of their sons would be in ministry and here I was fully trained for ministry. Surely, God deserves to be trusted for His word will always come to pass. His promises are always fulfilled in His time and not our time. God is never in a hurry to fulfil his promises for nothing will ever happen until what He purposes to do has been fully done. There is no delay with God. It's us who work on Chronos time when in fact, He will be awaiting to accomplish his purposes in His "Kairos" (God's) time.

As I write this book, I am the Founder and Senior Pastor of Harvest of Souls Ministries UK with other branches in Liberia, West Africa and Zimbabwe, Southern Africa. I am a testimony and a mystery to my parents that God gives and keeps His promises to all that fear and trust in Him.

It pays for the inferior to embrace the terms and conditions of the superior in order to enjoy the benefits of the superior.

To put a seal to this chapter, I will close with Hebrews 7:7 (ESV*), "It is beyond dispute that the inferior is blessed by the superior".* It is always the superior/greater that has something to give and he determines the terms and conditions for the inferior/lessor. It is the inferior that is at an advantage because he/she has it all to benefit when the superior might be giving it all to the inferior.

Amen.

CHAPTER 9: WE MAY FAIL GOD, BUT GOD CANNOT FAIL US

Allow me to take you back a bit. When I graduated in November 1983 with a BA degree in Bible/Theology from ICI, Brussels, Belgium; I applied to be a pastor in one of the affluent Pentecostal organizations in Zimbabwe, in Harare (The organization will remain anonymous because I want to maintain its spiritual integrity). When I was interviewed and recruited, my salary/allowance was never discussed with me neither did I ask nor was I inquisitive about it.

Having served for at least one month of January 1984, I was shocked to receive in a sealed khaki envelope a salary of $26.00. This was far too low than the money I was getting in my part-time employment while I was still training. At that moment, in the Provincial Office, I failed to see myself being able to budget anything with such a meagre income. Without having made a single stride outside the office, I immediately tendered my resignation with immediate effect. My resignation was immediately received and accepted, and I left the office.

I admit and confess that as a human, I was angry with God for calling me into ministry. I failed to trust in Him. I failed to realise at the time that there were some in ministry at the time who were started on the same salary and were serving God. I resigned because I failed to see my future on such a meagre salary/allowance. I failed to see God in all this. At face value, it was a mockery of my education and profession to have received $26.00. I trusted in my education and qualifications more than I could trust in the providence of God who keeps His promises.

By 7.45 am Zimbabwe time, I was at the recruitment office of the Ministry of Higher Education. By 8am, my appointment as a science teacher at Glen View1 High School was fully processed and I was asked urgently to report to the High School. By end of the day, I was already employed on a very lucrative salary. I was confident that I was able to continue to financially support my young siblings in their education as well as save money to marry my fiancé, Lucy.

Since the day I left the Provincial office, I was on a pastoral sabbatical period for seven years serving as an ordinary church member, although my local pastor recognised my qualification and used me to the benefit of the body of Christ. I became the scorn of ministry to some as they saw me as a man who was covetous and had thought that ministry was a lucrative enterprise. For seven years, the church leadership had lost hope that I had ever had a calling and would one day come back and serve as a Pastor. I too didn't envisage myself coming back into pastoral ministry for the salaries were still very low. I had completely failed God. I had failed to trust in Him. I had leaned on my own understanding. I had failed to commit all ways unto Him. I trusted in myself, my education, and my professional qualifications. But while I completely failed God and delayed my calling; God never failed me nor rejected me. He kept His eye on me and sustained me since He knew that I will one day come back to serve Him.

Then came God's calling again to come back to ministry and still at such low income. I tried all things to resist the calling like Jonah in the Bible who tried everything to resist his calling to go to

Nineveh. Amid my struggle to accept the calling, the Holy Spirit gave me a scripture in 1Thessalonians 5:24 which says, *"The one who calls you is faithful, and he will do it"*. The Holy Spirit assured me that my welfare was going to be taken care of by God if I accepted the calling back into ministry.

On that word, I succumbed to the second calling of God to come back into ministry, but I faced very stiff resistance from the then church leadership. They turned down my application on the basis that they thought I did not have a calling since I had left ministry on the grounds of low pay, and nothing then had significantly changed. By then I had changed my profession from the Ministry of Higher Education to the Ministry of Justice, Legal and Parliamentary Affairs. I had tendered my required three calendar months' notice to resign. Three days to my notice period, I again checked with the church leadership if they had reconsidered my application as that was my last window period to revoke my resignation and the church leadership summoned me to the Provincial Offices to personally tell me that I had no calling on my life. I recall speaking nasty words of frustration to my church leader and said, "If God is calling me and you say I don't have a calling; yet we both claim to have the same Holy Spirit, then it means, one of us has a demon. You will not see me in your office again". And so, I left.

> ◉
>
> In life there are gruesome times that you find yourself hard pressed between a rock and a hard place.

I was downcast in my spirit. The church leadership like I did before was now failing God, but God was not failing on them. I was now between a rock and a hard place. My colleagues at work wanted to know what greener pastures I was up to. I was left stuck with nothing to say even at a ministry farewell party which was scheduled for the last notice day. But God is faithful. He told me never to revoke my resignation. Three months after my resignation, I had completely lost hope that I will again join the pastoral ministry, but God had not lost hope on me. The church leadership had lost hope on me, but God had not lost hope on me and them.

I remember speaking to my wife and agreeing that I revert to the transport business since we owned trucks. I became a full-time lorry driver. It was not until one day, the same previous church leader whom I had had an uncomfortable encounter with came after me to my rural home to beg me to come back into ministry because God had told him that I should come back to ministry.

To cut the long story short, since the day I finally accepted the calling to come back into ministry, God had been faithful to His word. He has always supplied all my needs according to His riches in His glory. What I lack at times are wants but as far as needs are concerned, God supplies all of them in mysterious ways. God has never failed me. He has been always faithful to His word and promises.

Psalms 23:1 says, *"The Lord is my shepherd, I shall not want".* This Psalm has become my favourite verse together with 1 Thessalonians 5:24 which says, *"He who calls you is faithful; he will surely do it".* God promised to bless me, provide for my needs, protect me, and preserve me and until this day, God is still faithful to His word and promises. He has kept His promises to me without fail. I have seen the faithfulness of God ever since I came back to ministry until now. Goodness and mercy are surely

I might have failed God on many occasions, but God has never failed me.

following me, and I have now vowed to dwell in the house of the Lord serving Him with all my heart.

To conclude this chapter, all I can say is that God deserves to be trusted because of what He has always proved himself to be. He keeps His promises to those who trust in Him. The basis of trust as stated in this book is the ability to keep or fulfil promises. The Lord demonstrated that ability throughout scriptures and various testimonies of people.

Therefore, King Solomon was right in giving advice to his dear son in Proverbs 3:5-6 to *"Trust in the Lord with all your heart and lean not on your own understanding. In all your ways, acknowledge Him and He shall direct your paths".* The Apostle Paul writing to the Corinthian church says in 2 Corinthians 1:20 "For all the promises of God in him (Christ Jesus) are yea, and in him Amen, unto the glory of God by us". The 2nd "P" is God's Promises and indeed, God keeps His promises to those who trust in Him. Therefore, He deserves to be trusted. We may fail God, but He will not fail us.

Amen.

CHAPTER 10: THE PROVISIONS OF THE LORD

I have already established the fact that *"It Pays to Trust the LORD as a Principle to Respond to God"* because He exist for that purpose, and He keeps His promises so that He can be trusted.

Politicians in every political spectrum, campaign on a premise that they can deliver on their promises to the electorate. They will give a list of promises that they will provide in the best interest of their constituents. They capitalize on the needs of their communities in their local constituents. However, some politicians over-promise and yet under-deliver on their promises to their electorate. When that happens, they will lose the trust of their electorate in the next elections.

But in the spiritual arena, those that trust in the Lord will never be let down if God has promised to provide anything for them. The Lord will always provide whatever he promises. He proved it in all generations.

> The Lord deserves to be trusted because He can always provide for the NEEDS of His people.

The human philosophy

Abraham Harold Maslow, a renowned American psychologist argued that people can only reach the "Aha!" moment in their lives in self-actualization when their five levels of their needs have been met as shown in Fig.1 below:

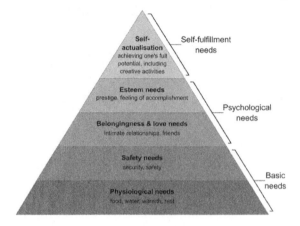

FIGURE 1 ABRAHAM HAROLD MASLOW'S HIERARCHY OF NEEDS

"In his major works, Motivation and Personality (1954) and Toward a Psychology of Being (1962), Maslow argues that each person has a hierarchy of needs that must be satisfied, ranging from basic physiological requirements to love, esteem, and, finally, self-actualization. As each need is satisfied, the next higher level in the emotional hierarchy dominates conscious functioning. Maslow argues that healthy people are self-actualizers because they satisfy the highest psychological needs, fully integrating the components of their personality or self."i.

In other words, Maslow is saying that people are mostly happy (which I called the Aha! Moment) when their needs are satisfied. It is human nature to trust anything and anyone who can satisfy human needs. This is generally our natural human philosophy of life.

Figure 1 shows that physiological needs like food, water, shelter, warmth, air, and rest are the most basic human needs that must be provided to people as the first step to their happiness in life. Anyone who can provide them will earn the trust of the people. Now, the Lord our God can supply all the physiological needs as stated in the below scripture.

> Joel 2:21-27 *"Fear not, O land; be glad and rejoice, or the LORD has done great things! Fear not, you beasts of the field, or the pastures of the wilderness are green; the tree bears its fruit; the fig tree and vine give their full yield. "Be glad, O children of Zion, and rejoice in the LORD your God, for he has given the early rain for your vindication; he has poured down for you, abundant rain, the early and the latter rain, as before. "The threshing floors shall be full of grain; the vats shall overflow with wine and oil.*

I will restore to you the years that the swarming locust has eaten, the hopper, the destroyer, and the cutter, my great army, which I sent among you.

> *"You shall eat in plenty and be satisfied, and praise the name of the LORD your God, who has dealt wondrously with you. And my people shall never again be put to shame. You shall know that I am in the midst of Israel, and that I am the LORD your God and there is none else. And my people shall never again be put to shame".*

God makes the beasts in the fields glad by providing them with green pastures and water to drink while he makes people happy by giving them the early and later rains and making their trees bear fruit and fill their granaries with grain.

The preceding scripture is very clear that it pays off to trust in the Lord because He can provide for all our basic physiological needs.

God can satisfy the human needs

Physiological needs

With all the confidence that I have in the Lord Jesus Christ, I can assuredly say that the Lord is able to provide all the five levels of the human needs as stated by Maslow in Fig.1 above. The Bible is full of instances when God was able to meet the physiological needs of his people that trusted in Him.

First, God provided a garden with all manner of fruits to the first people Adam and his wife Eve in the garden of Eden (Genesis 2:8-9).

Second, in Exodus 16:33-34, we are told that there is a pot of manna (heavenly bread) that was symbolic to the nation of Israel that God provided them with food for forty years as they journeyed in the wilderness.

Third, in 2 Kings 7, we have an account of a great famine in the land of Samaria to an extent that certain women agreed to take turns to kill, cook and eat their children. But at the word of Elisha the prophet; God was going to be gracious with his people; there was going to be plenty of food by the next day in the city of Samaria. Indeed, a miracle did take place in twenty-four hours and there was plenty of food in Samaria.

All these instances are good examples that God can provide the physiological needs of his people as defined by Maslow. In Matthew 4 and Luke 4 we have similar accounts where Jesus Christ was tempted by the devil to turn stones into bread and feed himself since he was hungry after 40 days and nights of no food and drink. Jesus refused to do that miracle as a show-off and thereby tempting God. It appeared as if he was unable to do such a miracle to provide himself with food. However, in his ministry, we have two accounts where Jesus fed 5000- and 4000-men excluding women and children from a few loaves of bread and a few fish (Mt 14:13-21; 15:32-39). His first miracle at Cana in Galilee as recorded by John the gospel was turning water into wine (John 2). So, Jesus is quite capable of providing food to those who can trust in Him. Remember in John chapter two, Jesus acted and performed the miracle in response to His mother who had demonstrated her faith in the ability of her son to provide for the needs of the people at a wedding party. Each time Jesus saw people, He was moved with compassion as He saw their physical needs of health and hunger. The Bible says that He provided for all their needs.

Safety needs

On another occasion, the security of a desperate woman who was caught in the act of adultery was at stake as her accusers were wielding stones ready to stone her to death (John 8:1-11). Jesus responded to her accusers by writing the law down asking each of them if there was anyone who had not sinned to first cast a stone at her. All the people dispersed as they realised that they too had broken the law. When Jesus was left with the woman, he let her go freely but advised her never to sin again. According to Maslow's law, Jesus as Lord can be trusted because He can guarantee the safety of those that can come to Him for protection and provision. The adulterous woman found safety in Jesus.

In the book of Matthew 14:22-33, again we have a story where the safety of the disciples sailing by boat was at stake as they were tossed at sea by vicious storms. Jesus came to the disciples in a boat walking on top of the water. When he arrived, he calmed the storm and the disciples felt safe. They came to him, worshipped him and acknowledged him indeed, as the Son of God.

Belonging and Love needs

Oftentimes, Jesus was accused by the religious leaders of his day for being friendly with the outcasts of the community (Luke

15:1-2) and for dining with them in their houses (Luke 19:1-10). According to Maslow's hierarchy of needs, Jesus provided friendship and connected with   outcasts and unusual people far from what was expected of the Messiah. Jesus embraced all people regardless of their condition including those with infectious diseases like leprosy.

One of the main teachings of Jesus Christ is *"Love others in the same way as you would love yourself"*. He demonstrated that He loved people by attending invitations to wedding parties and dinners as well as visiting ordinary and prominent people in their homes like Zacchaeus [John 2:1-2; 12:1-2; Luke 19:5].

Esteem needs

When society rejects you, it destroys your self-esteem. When society casts you out, you feel unworthy, you lose your dignity as a human. Jesus was a friend to the marginalised people of the society and often He would go where they were to help them and give them a sense of worthiness.

In Mark 5:1-20, we have a story of a man who was visited by Jesus in the cemetery where he lived because he was being tormented by unclean spirits. Jesus visited him to cast out the unclean spirits. When the unclean spirits left the man, he got dressed up and he was back in his right senses. His humanity was restored, and he went back to the community and enjoyed life just like any other person.

Another story is recorded in Luke 17:11-19. Jesus passed through an area where there were ten lepers. These men were to keep their social distance from people lest they spread their infectious disease. When they cried for help, Jesus healed them, and He asked them to go and show themselves to the priests who were to declare them clean and allow them to go and mix with other people.

In the Old Testament, in 2 Kings 5:1-14, we have a story of Naaman the leper who came from Syria to Israel to a prophet to be healed. After being told to dip seven times into the Jordan river, he was healed, and his skin was like that of a young boy. He returned home rejoicing. It is the Lord who can restore our self-esteem when every sense of worthiness is gone. This is the reason why King Solomon urged his son to trust in the Lord.

Jesus should be trusted because, in his physical days on earth, he was able to satisfy the psychological needs of people by strengthening their self-esteem as he made them feel accepted once again to communities that previously rejected them. Just being around Jesus made people feel a sense of self-actualization as they began to unleash their potential in life.

Self-Actualization

It is the Lord who can only bring us to the highest moments of happiness without regret. Having given victory to a young man called David against a giant Goliath, David came back home happy and being celebrated by people and women danced and sang songs of praise to him [1Samuel 18:5 -7]. People can only reach the self-actualization "Aha! Moments" when something has happened that brings them great joy. When God gave Israel the victory over their enemies through David, peoples' spirits were uplifted.

It is only God who can uplift peoples' spirits and cause them to reach the Aha! Moments in life.

When King Solomon encouraged his son in Proverbs 3:5 to trust in the Lord, he was saying that it's only God who can bring anyone to an "aha! moments in life" if you trust in Him.

If anyone is to be trusted, I have already said that someone should have earned the trust. God by what he did through Jesus

Christ is sufficient evidence that he deserves to be trusted. He provided a way in the Red Sea and manna in the wilderness and water from the rock to the people that trusted him as he led them. All this demonstrates that the Lord can provide for our human needs and hence he deserves to be trusted. Trust in the Lord with all your heart and lean not on your understanding. This is sound advice.

In a nutshell, physiological needs [food, water, warmth, healing and rest] must be met first according to Maslow's hierarchy of needs if ever a person is to be happy or trust anyone. The Lord God provided for these basic needs as summarised below:

FOOD

Jesus Christ fed 5000 men in addition to all the women and children – Mt 14:13- 21

Jesus Christ fed 4000 men in addition to all the women and children – Mt 15:32-39

Elisha fed 100 people with 20 loaves – 2Kings 4:42-44

WATER

Moses provided water to drink at Massah and Meribah to the Israelites from a rock – Ex. 17:1-7; Neh. 9:15

Isaiah appealed to the Israelites to come and get water freely – Isa. 55:1

Jesus Christ pleads with people to come to him and drink so that they thirst no more – Jn 7:37-38; 4:13-15

WARMTH (Shelter & Clothing)

God covered the nakedness of Adam and Eve – Gen 3:10-11

God preserved the clothes of Israelites for 40 years – Dt 8:4

God acted as the shelter to the psalmists – Ps 61:3-4

God gives warmth – Haggai 1:6

HEALING

God provides healing by the wounds of Jesus Christ – Isa 53:5

Moses prayed for Meriam to be healed of leprosy – Nu 12:13

Naaman the leper was healed by Elisha – 2Kings 5:10-14

King Hezekiah was sick unto death, and he was healed – Isa 38

Jesus healed many people of their sicknesses and diseases – Lk 4:40; Mt 15:30

Jesus healed the woman with an issue of blood – Mt 9:20-22

God's desire that we be of good health – 3Jn 1:2

REST

Jesus made an appeal to the people to come unto him; all of them that they were weary and heavy-laden of heart – Mt 11:28

God gave the land rest or peace for 80 years – Judges 3:30

Jesus Christ can fully be trusted because in his ministry while on earth he was able to provide for the first level of basic needs according to Abraham's Maslow hierarchy of needs. He can also be trusted because he was able to fulfil the second level of the hierarchy of needs which are the Safety needs as highlighted below:

SECURITY

"The safety needs can be summarized by including the security of the body, of employment, of resources, of the family, of health, and of property that can come in the form of personal security, financial security, and overall health and wellbeing"[ii].

Jesus Christ was concerned mainly with the security of his disciples and so he prayed to the father for them. John 17:11-13 *"And now I am no more in the world, but these are in the world, and I come to you. Holy Father keep through your own name those* *whom you have given me, that they may be one, as we are. While I was with them in the world, **I kept them in your name: those that you gave me I have kept, and none of them is lost,** but the son of perdition; that the scripture might be fulfilled. And now come I to you; and these things I speak in the world, that they might have my joy fulfilled in themselves".*

The reason Jesus Christ came walking on top of the water to calm the storms was that he was concerned with the security and safety of his disciples as they were tossed by the terrible storms of the sea – Mt 14:22-33. When Jesus Christ was about to be arrested by the Chief Priests in the Garden of Gethsemane again, he was concerned with the security and safety of his disciples and hence he asked the arrestors to let his disciples first go away unharmed – Jn 18:8-9.

In the book of Revelation, there is an appeal by Jesus Christ to the church of Laodicea to come to him and get true riches – Rev 3:18. The Psalmist acknowledged the security and safety he finds in God in Psalms 18:1-2 *"I will love you, O LORD, my strength. The LORD is my rock, and my fortress, and my deliverer; my God, my strength, in whom I will trust; my shield, and the horn of my salvation, and my high tower".*

Personal Testimonies

God supplied our need

There was a time in my ministry when one day my wife and I woke up with virtually nothing to give to our children for food except half of a loaf which we asked the kids to share as breakfast. We took our kids to church and closed the doors to pray for God's provision. After the prayer, we let our children go with the confidence that God had heard our prayers.

Indeed, God had heard our prayers. A woman felt restless in her spirit while she was at work in Harare, Zimbabwe. The Spirit was urging her to quickly go and buy groceries for the pastor and deliver them as soon as possible. During her lunch break, she managed to buy the groceries and drove seven miles to offload them at our house. In a span of four hours, my children had already seen the provision of the Lord as they were being asked to carry the groceries into the house. It pays to trust in the Lord.

Driving on an empty tank

Again, in the ministry, while I was a Pastor at the Mutorashanga mines, Zimbabwe, the Lord on several occasions miraculously provided fuel to our Citroën GS Club car, vehicle registration number 279-031T (pictured here), whenever it was empty while I was in the master's service, driving among the Mutorashanga Assemblies preaching the gospel of salvation. There was only one filling station in all the mines and it was at Mutorashanga. The fuel would be on empty while we were several miles away from the filling station and our car would drive on an empty tank until we could find a filling station. There  wasn't a day that we got stranded on the road because of fuel. God can supernaturally fuel a car if you trust in Him. It pays to trust in the LORD. *(The picture above shows the vintage car that I have kept at Gweshe Township, Chiweshe, Zimbabwe in memory of the mighty acts of God to his dear servant).*

> As long as we kept ourselves trusting God in everything we were doing, we always saw the hand and faithfulness of God's provision.

This miracle was a fulfilment of God's word that He would provide for all our needs.

God knows your physical address

Another miracle that happened while we were still Pastors at Mutorashanga between 1991 and 1995 was that we were surprised to receive suitcases of clothing items for the entire family from an unknown group in the United States of America. During their prayer meetings, the group was told by the Holy Spirit to buy clothes for me, and my family and they were given each of my family members clothes and shoe sizes as well as my postal address. My family and I were surprised one day to receive a note from the Post office to come and collect parcels. The parcels were suitcases of brand-new clothes from the USA from a group of people unknown to us. The clothes had correct sizes for each of my family members. This miracle happened within the same period of the Citroën GS Club empty tank miracle cited earlier.

Jesus said, *my sheep know my voice and I know my sheep by name.* Because He knew us and what we needed, He provided for our needs even with far distant people whom we do not know even to this day. It pays to trust in the Lord.

Chapter 11: The Protection of the Lord

Psalms 125:1-2 *"They that trust in the LORD shall be as mount Zion, which cannot be removed, but abides forever. As the mountains are round about Jerusalem, so the LORD is round about his people from this time forth even forever".*

Oh! What a mouthful statement that is being declared by the Psalmist. "They that trust in the Lord shall be as mount Zion which cannot be removed but abides forever". The message is not for everyone but for "those that trust in the Lord". There are benefits to be enjoyed by "those that trust in the

> What is so unique with those "that trust in the Lord"? They are unmovable and unshakable.

Lord". Those that have their confidence, their reliability, their dependence, and their assurance in God have something that others don't have.

Divine protection

The Psalmist has an answer. Those that trust in the Lord have divine protection. They are like mount Zion which cannot be moved. With all the strength that people have, all forces put together, none of them can move an inch of a mountain. Enemies below the valley or on the mountain skirts cannot overpower those on the higher altitude. Those on the mountain see it all and have it all. Their defence is so strong that none can dare come to them and attack them willy-nilly.

>
>
> Those that trust in the Lord are never perturbed by any situation.

The defence of those that trust in the Lord is so strong that the devil with all his combined forces thinks twice before he can launch his attack. They abide in the Lord forever without any fear or distress.

He sets a hedge of protection

> There is divine protection to those that trust in the Lord.

God always puts a hedge of protection against his people. The Lord guarantees maximum security to those that trust in him. Even Christ at one time in his prayer in John 17 had to say, *"Father, none of those that you put in my hands have I lost".* He kept them in his name. Christ's hands serve as a hedge of protection against the roaring lion that moves around seeking whom to devour.

Satan acknowledged that fact when one day he was found among the sons of God before the throne of grace. When he was asked if ever, he observed the Lord's servant Job in his wandering to and from the earth; he replied and said that God had put a hedge of protection upon Job, his family and property. Satan didn't just want the awesome protection that he saw upon Job and his family. It hurts him to the

> He will never leave our souls vulnerable to the destruction of Satan.

core when he sees how God protects his people. He always wishes if that hedge of protection is removed, and he is given permission to vex the saints. But God is faithful.

God acts as a fortress.

Psalm 125:1-2 is a great testimony by the Psalmists. Mountains unlike valleys provide a very good defence system to the military. They give an added advantage to the troops to gain victory. God acts as a fortress to those who trust in him. His people are never terrified or dismayed by their opponents. God shields and protects his people.

King David understood the protection of the Lord when he penned Psalms 23:4 *"Yea, though I walk through the valley of the shadow of death, I will fear no evil: for you are with me; your rod and your staff they comfort me".*

What is interesting is the fact that the writers of the book of Psalms were not writing stories out of the blues. Psalms are songs or poems. Songs or poems are always sung or narrated from experiences of life, and they are not mere fantasies. From the Psalms quoted above, it is clear that the Psalmists never hesitated to state the protection that God gives to his people. The Lord God protects his own people.

Victory belongs to God

King David in his youthful days, was a shepherd boy. In his account to King Saul as he wanted to go and fight with the uncircumcised Philistine Goliath, David showed us that twice his life was in danger of a lion and a bear when they wanted to attack his sheep in the pastures (1Samuel 17:34-37). But it was the Lord whom he trusted that delivered him from the paws of a lion and a bear.

David, by the same faith, trusted that the same God who had delivered him from the mouth and paws of a lion and a bear was going to deliver into his hands Goliath and Israel was going to win the battle in the name of the Lord. Indeed, Goliath was defeated by David not with sophisticated weaponry but with a sling and a stone.

> *1Samuel 17:45-47, Then David said to the Philistine, "You come to me with a sword and with a spear and with a javelin, but I come to you in the name of the LORD of hosts, the God of the armies of Israel, whom you have defied. This day the LORD will deliver you into my hand, and I will strike you down and cut off your head. And I will give the dead bodies of the host of the Philistines this day to the birds of the air and to the wild beasts of the earth, that all the earth may know that there is a God in Israel, and that all this assembly may know that the LORD saves not with sword and spear. For the battle is the LORD'S, and he will give you into our hand."*

In another incident in 2 Chronicles 20, we have an account of King Jehoshaphat being under attack from the Moabites and Ammonites. When the word reached him that the great armies were coming to attack him, the bible says that he sought the Lord and proclaimed a fast throughout all Judah. They prayed and trusted the Lord to bring them deliverance.

God sent a word through prophet Jahaziel to Jehoshaphat and all Judah:

> *(2 Chronicles 20:17) "You shall not need to fight in this battle: set yourselves, stand you still, and see the salvation of the LORD with you, O Judah and Jerusalem: fear not, nor be dismayed; tomorrow go out against them: for the LORD will be with you".*
>
> 2 Chronicles 20:20-22 *"And they rose early in the morning and went forth into the wilderness of Tekoa: and*

*as they went forth, Jehoshaphat stood and said, Hear me,
O Judah, and you inhabitants of Jerusalem; Believe in the
LORD your God, so shall you be established; believe his
prophets, so shall you prosper. And when he had
consulted with the people, he appointed singers unto the
LORD, that should praise the beauty of holiness, as they
went out before the army, and to say, Praise the LORD;
for his mercy endures forever. And when they began to
sing and to praise, the LORD set ambushes against the
children of Ammon, Moab, and mount Seir, who were
come against Judah; and they were defeated".*

The Lord protected his people from the hands of the enemies
because they trusted in him. It pays to trust in the Lord.

God frustrates the plans of the enemies.

In Exodus 14, we have the story of Israel crossing the Red Sea
and the Egyptians were pursuing them. The Bible says in Exodus
14:19-20:

*"And the angel of God, who went before the camp of
Israel, moved and went behind them; and the pillar of the
cloud went from before their face, and stood behind
them: And it came between the camp of the Egyptians and
the camp of Israel; and it was a cloud and darkness to
them, but it gave light by night to these: so that the one
came not near the other all the night".*

The angel of the Lord protected the Israelites from the
Egyptians by preventing them from coming near to them. When
the enemy seeks to pursue those that trust in the Lord, all their
plans will be frustrated by God such that he will not succeed in
overcoming the saints.

When the Lord God says "Fear not, don't be afraid" he means what he says. God has all the wisdom, knowledge, and power to protect his own. Imagine, an angel that was leading the children of Israel in their journey just came behind them as they were crossing the Red Sea and the mighty armies of Pharaoh were kept at a distance until Moses stretched his hand and the waters covered the armies of Pharaoh and drowned them.

When Shadrach, Meshach and Abednego were thrown into a burning fiery furnace by Nebuchadnezzar in Babylon for the simple reason that they had refused to bow down and worship his image, the Lord God came into the burning fiery furnace and quenched the heat of the fire so that not even the smell of smoke came onto their clothes.

Daniel 3:26-30, *Then Nebuchadnezzar came near to the door of the burning fiery furnace; he declared, "Shadrach, Meshach, and Abednego, servants of the Most High God, come out, and come here!" Then Shadrach, Meshach, and Abednego came out from the fire. And the satraps, the prefects, the governors, and the king's counsellors gathered together and saw that the fire had not had any power over the bodies of those men. The hair of their heads was not singed, their cloaks were not harmed, and no smell of fire had come upon them. Nebuchadnezzar answered and said, "Blessed be the God of Shadrach, Meshach, and Abednego, who has sent his angel and delivered his servants, who trusted in him, and set aside the king's command, and yielded up their bodies rather than serve and worship any god except their own God. Therefore, I make a decree: Any people, nation, or language that speaks anything against the God of Shadrach, Meshach, and Abednego shall be torn limb from limb, and their houses laid in ruins, for there is no other god who is able to rescue in this way." Then the king promoted Shadrach, Meshach, and Abednego in the province of Babylon.*

While it is a fact that the church can always suffer persecution and some members of the body of Christ become martyrs that should not obliterate the fact that God protects his own people. James the brother of John, sons of Zebedee, one of the early disciples to be called by Jesus was a martyr by the hand of King Herod in Acts 12:1-2. At the same time, Peter was imprisoned with the hope of executing him after Easter (Passover). But the angel of the Lord came by night and released Peter from prison (Acts 12:5-11).

It may appear as if God allows evil to triumph over the saints just as it happened in the case of Job whom Satan attacked (Job 1 & 2). God allows that only if it proves to the devil that the martyrs are the faithful, God-loving servants who love him dearly more than their lives. To such people, God gives sufficient grace to go through such hardships so that in the end, God gets the glory. Amid pain and affliction, a Christian will always get encouragement from Psalms 46:10 *"Be still and know that I am God: I will be exalted among the nations, I will be exalted in the earth".*

Psalms 23:4 *"Yea, though I walk through the valley of the shadow of death, I will fear no evil: for you are with me; your rod and your staff they comfort me".*

1 Samuel 17:47 *"...the LORD saves not with sword and spear: for the battle is the LORD's..."* Throughout generations the Lord always proved that he could fight for his own and can save them. The Lord protects his people.

My Personal Testimony

Allow me to share my testimony to substantiate the fact that the Lord protects those who trust in him. In my pastoral ministry, the devil on several occasions tried to terminate my life and my wife and family.

Live rooster with spells

On one occasion, one church member (possibly due to hatred, jealousy and envy of the Pastor's family) sent her child with a live rooster for the pastor and family to kill and enjoy. Early on a Sunday morning, about 6.30 am, there was a knock on my door and our maid who was just sweeping the courtyard outside was knocking to tell us that we were blessed with a gift of a white rooster. We asked her to put it in our outside fowl run. My wife and I didn't ask to see the rooster when we woke up because we were getting ready for our 10am morning service. On that day, the Lord used me mightily in preaching his word. There was healing and deliverance in church after the sermon. God's presence during the church service was just extraordinarily awesome and supernatural.

After the church service, I took my wife, the vice chairman and his wife on our regular home visits on a Sunday after church service. About 9pm on that Sunday, when I was about to drop my vice chairman and his wife at their home, my wife recalled that there was a rooster that we had been given early in the morning. However, she told our vice chairman about the dream she had had previously in the week and my vice chairman immediately said, "Let's go back to church. That rooster is intended to bring evil spells on the family. You should not touch it, lest you go mad". Indeed, this was a revelation of the Lord. The rooster had evil enchantments upon it.

When we came to the fowl run, the vice chairman went and picked the rooster and we drove off to go and throw it away from home. When I had driven the car just less than 100 metres away, the live white rooster died suddenly in the hands of the vice chairman. We were all shocked how a live healthy white rooster can all of a sudden be dead. I then drove about 200 metres and my vice chairman got out of the car in a nearby bush and threw it away.

It my wife's dream, she had seen a rooster being given to us. When she slaughtered it so that she can cook it, she immediately went psyche. That was the reason she remembered the dream and the rooster that had come early in the morning. Brothers and sisters, it pays to listen to God and take heed of His warnings. It pays to trust in the Lord as a principle of responding to Him.

A week later, the woman who had given us the rooster knew that nothing had happened to us. When she came for a women's midweek meeting, she cheerfully asked repeatedly my wife, if ever she had slaughtered the rooster and cooked it. My wife replied "yes" to her. She replied, "I don't think so". My wife repeatedly said, "surely, surely, we ate the rooster, and it was tasty and delicious. Thank you so much for your kindness". But her looks were disfigured and unhappy and she went away.

From that day the woman had to put on a shy face and could not look eye to eye with me or my wife whenever she came for church services and whenever we visited her home on our pastoral home visits. She was even surprised that we still had to include her in our regular home visits and would still eat in her home. Brothers and sisters, God protects his own if you put your trust in Him.

My family had divine protection from the hand of the enemy who wanted to destroy me and my family simply because she hated the gospel I preached. The Apostle Paul writing to his son in the Lord Timothy in 2 Timothy 4:3-5 said, *"For the time is coming when people will not endure sound teaching but having itching ears, they will accumulate for themselves teachers to suit their own passions and will turn away from listening to the truth and wander off into myths. As for you, always be sober-minded, endure suffering, do the work of an evangelist, fulfil your ministry".* The Lord vindicated me and my family from the wile schemes of the devil. The Lord protects His own with a mighty hand.

Poisoned food for the Pastor

As if that was not enough, on another occasion, there was a funeral and we had just come back from the cemetery. I always made sure to come back into the house where the coffin lay in state to pray and cleanse the house. On that day, I did as usual and made my prayers.

God had warned us not to eat any food on that day. So, my wife and I together with my junior associate, Pastor Kuyedza, immediately made our way out of the house as if we were hurrying to go somewhere. We were stopped by one lady because our food had been prepared for us to eat. I insisted that we were in a hurry, and we were not sitting down to eat. We were implored to even carry the food and eat later but we denied it. The woman who was asking us to eat the food did not know that another woman had poisoned the food.

God can frustrate and bring to nothing the plans of the enemy as he protects those that love Him and trust in Him.

A week later, we were told by some women that the food that was meant for us at the funeral, when it was taken back to a group of ladies who had served it; they were ordered not to eat that food and were asked to throw it away by a certain woman. Later, the thrown away food was eaten by a dog. The dog became unwell and died few hours thereafter. When the other women saw what had happened, they were grateful to God that the pastors had not eaten the poisoned food.

I trust in the Lord because I have seen his hand of protection over my life and family and the church at large. My faith is never shaken because I know who I have believed. I am strong in the Lord as mount Zion that cannot be removed but abides forever (Psalm 125:1-2). I will share with you other testimonies as I make progress in this book.

I agree with the submission of the author of Proverbs 3:5, *"Trust in the Lord with all your heart and lean not on your understanding. In all your ways acknowledge Him"*. If my wife and I ever relied on our own understanding, I could not have been alive to write this book today. The devil has always been after our lives, but he has always failed because of the divine protection over our lives.

God is steadfast in His love and mercy, and He always lives to protect and preserve his own people who trust and fear Him. Like what King David said in Psalm 23, He does so for His name's sake. Our Good Shepherd has a good reputation for protection. He protects His own. Fear not if you have taken the God of Abraham, Isaac and Jacob as your refuge and a rock on which to stand. Fear not, if you have chosen the rejected stone by the builders which has become a chief cornerstone of your life. Fear not because the one who has called you, neither sleeps nor slumber but watches over you to protect and preserve you. His name is faithful and wonderful. He will protect you from this day forth and forever if you keep on trusting in Him.

I would conclude this section with a testimony by Martin Luther King Jr – "If I had sneezed" from an extract of The New York Times by Alexandra S. Levine, Jan. 12.2017[iii].

"It was Sept. 20, 1958. Dr King was at Blumstein's, a store on West 125th Street in Harlem, where he was signing copies of his first book, "Stride Toward Freedom: The Montgomery Story."

In walked a woman — dressed to the nines — presumably for an autograph from the 29-year-old civil rights activist. But hidden beneath her lovely outfit were a letter opener and a loaded .25-caliber pistol.

The woman, Izola Ware Curry, approached Dr King, drew the letter opener from her purse and stabbed him in the chest.

Dr King could not immediately remove the blade; it was too close to his heart. He was told not to move an inch, not to speak. He was rushed to Harlem Hospital for emergency surgery.

The doctors later told him that any sudden movement — so much as a sneeze — could have cost him his life.

The frightening, near-fatal New York episode later became a point of inspiration in Dr King's "I've Been to the Mountaintop" address, which he delivered on April 3, 1968, in Memphis, the day before he was assassinated.

Ahead of Dr King's birthday on Sunday, we wanted to share excerpts from the legendary speech:

"I, too, am happy that I didn't sneeze."

"Because if I had sneezed, I wouldn't have been around here in 1960, when students all over the South started sitting-in at lunch counters."

"If I had sneezed, I wouldn't have been around here in 1961, when we decided to take a ride for freedom and ended segregation in interstate travel."

"If I had sneezed, I wouldn't have been here in 1963, when the black people of Birmingham, Ala., aroused the conscience of this nation and brought into being the Civil Rights Bill."

"If I had sneezed, I wouldn't have had a chance later that year, in August, to try to tell America about a dream that I had had."

"I'm so happy that I didn't sneeze."

God protected Rev Dr Martin Luther King Jr by stopping him to just sneeze. With pain from stabbing, instinct would cause one to pull out the knife, but the Lord God prevented him from taking such an action. Those who trust in the Lord, the Lord will miraculously protect them. It pays to trust in Lord. This is the reason why scriptures encourage us to trust in the Lord.

Amen

CHAPTER 12: THE PRESERVATION OF THE LORD

Trust in the Lord because the Lord God preserves life. God loves His creation and mankind is His creation. His love for His creation forces Him to do whatever it takes to preserve life. The enemy of life does everything within his power to destroy life, but the Lord God does all it takes to preserve and save a life.

This is the reason why John 3:16-18 says,

"For God so loved the world, that he gave his only Son, that whoever believes in him should not perish but have eternal life. For God did not send his Son into the world to condemn the world, but in order that the world might be saved through him. Whoever believes in him is not condemned, but whoever does not believe is condemned already, because he has not believed in the name of the only Son of God".

To preserve and save mankind, God had to send His only dear Son Jesus Christ into the world, to save the world so that the world might have eternal life. Christ came so that we might have life in abundance [John 10:10].

The dictionary definition of "preserve" is to maintain in its original or existing state or to treat or to prevent from decomposition. Restore can mean to bring back to a former, original, or normal condition. Combined, God is in the ministry and/or business of preserving and restoring souls and bringing them back into his glory.

Sin ruined mankind and we lost our divine glory. Romans 3:23 says, *"For all have sinned, and come short of the glory of God".* When Adam and Eve were first created by God, they were created in the image and likeness of God.

> Genesis 1:26-27 *"And God said, Let us make man in our image, after our likeness... So, God created man in his own image, in the image of God created he him; male and female created he them".*

Sin is a failure to comply with the instruction of God.

God is clothed in his glory. Glory is the beauty of his holiness, the power of his majesty and the splendour of his sovereignty. Adam and Eve were created clothed with the glory of God. Satan who disguised himself as a serpent at the time of temptation wanted to corrupt the holiness, majesty, and sovereignty of God's glory in mankind by evil. He tempted Adam and Eve to disobey God. Sin is disobedience to what God has said. Sin is a fall from the expected standard of holiness before God. God's standard of holiness is His glory. Therefore, sin is falling short of God's standard of holiness/glory [Romans 3:23]. Subsequently, man lost God's glory and became naked.

When the time to be visited by God approached, Adam and Eve realised that they had lost God's glory which was their covering and were afraid and embarrassed to meet with God. God's holiness/glory exposes man's shortcomings and nakedness. They also lost their dignity and dominion over all living creatures. They decided to hide from God's presence and attempted to substitute God's glory with a covering of fig tree leaves.

> Genesis 3:6-8 *"And when the woman saw that the tree was good for food, and that it was pleasant to the eyes, and a tree to be desired to make one wise, she took of the fruit thereof, and did eat, and gave also unto her husband with her; and he did eat. And the eyes of them both were opened, and they knew that they were naked; and they sewed fig leaves together and made themselves aprons. And they heard the voice of the LORD God walking in the garden in the cool of the day: and Adam and his wife hid themselves from the presence of the LORD God among the trees of the garden".*

When God saw that Adam and Eve had lost His glory, dignity and dominion, He had to kill an animal in the garden and provided its skins as a covering for man to substitute for his lost glory.

> Genesis 3:21 *"Unto Adam also and to his wife did the LORD God make coats of skins and clothed them".*

God clothed Adam and Eve with coats of skins as a way of preserving their souls. God restored their souls so that they may have fellowship with God once more through the shedding of animal blood and covering with skins. Folks, it pays to trust in the Lord because when you fall short of God's expectation, by His mercy, He will come and preserve and save your life. This is the understanding that King Solomon wanted his son to have and pursue in life.

However, at the time of the fall of man, the human body assumed the decomposition matter and it was destined for death at the end of life. The preservation and restoration of human beings were going to be in two phases namely the preservation/restoration of the soul and the preservation/restoration of the body. I will explain a little bit about this.

It is written in Isaiah 61:1-2:

> *"The spirit of the Lord GOD is upon me; because the LORD has anointed me to preach good tidings unto the meek; he has sent me to bind up the broken-hearted, to proclaim liberty to the captives, and the opening of the prison to them that are bound; To proclaim the acceptable year of the LORD, and the day of vengeance of our God; to comfort all that mourn".*

The prophet Isaiah was pointing to two phases of the emancipation of the human being from the adverse effects of sin that was now inherent in man. The first liberation is of the SOUL and the second liberation is of the BODY. However, a human being is a tripartite being meaning he is made up of Spirit, Soul and Body.

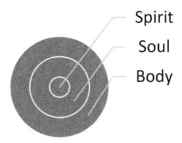

Figure 2 A Human being is tripartite

God first took the dirt or dust of the earth and made the body the lifeless body. He then breathed His Spirit or breath (Hebrew word is *ruach*) into the body through the nostrils. The fusion of the Spirit and the body forms the middle component which is the Soul. And a human being became a living soul and/or being.

Now, Jesus Christ is life. John 1:1-4 says, *"In the beginning was the Word, and the Word was with God, and the Word was God.*

The same was in the beginning with God. All things were made by him; and without him was not anything made that was made. In him was life; and the life was the light of men".

The gospel is good news. What is the good news? John 3:16-17 tells us the good news. *"For God so loved the world, that he gave his only begotten Son, that whosoever believes in him should not perish, but have everlasting life. For God sent not his Son into the world to condemn the world; but that the world through him might be saved".*

What the verses above imply is that it is not God's prerogative agenda that human beings should perish because of the inherent sinful nature in them. According to the Webster-Merriam dictionary, the word *"perish"* if used as an intransitive verb it can mean "to become destroyed or ruined or cease to exist"; it can also mean "to deteriorate or spoil". Used as a transitive verb it can mean "to cause to die". The verses imply that it is God's plan to preserve or restore the human being from being ruined or destroyed completely so that he ceases to exist.

The gospel introduces to human beings how we can be preserved or restored from annihilation. If we accept Jesus Christ as the means to our preservation and restoration, we shall be saved from utter destruction. If Jesus Christ is accepted by faith, he activates our dead souls by giving back a new spirit and we become a new creation.

2 Corinthians 5:17-18 says, *"Therefore, if any man be in Christ, he is a new creation: old things are passed away; behold, all things are become new. And all things are of God, who has reconciled us to himself by Jesus Christ, and has given to us the ministry of reconciliation".*

When Jesus Christ came, He declared his first mission in Luke 4:18-19 as He quoted Isaiah 61:1-2. His first mission was to pay for the price of the emancipation of the Soul. It is the soul that becomes poor when it loses the glory of God. It is the soul that is broken-hearted with the issues of life. It is the soul that has been taken captive by sin and needs to be liberated. It is the soul that has lost its vision of the Lord and is living in darkness. It is the soul that is oppressed by the devil through sin and needs liberation. It is the soul that yearns for the favour or grace of God. And it is aforesaid that Christ quoted that He was anointed to accomplish for human beings. This needed a higher price of blood without blemish. No other blood on earth was good enough to pay for the price. So, God sent his only Son to come and die to have the blood that could be sprinkled once and for all on the mercy seat of God so that human beings can be forgiven their sins and be reconciled with God and have their souls redeemed and saved.

This is the reason why the Hebrew people refer to him as the Messiah meaning Saviour. The other name would be Yeshua meaning "the Lord saves". This is the implication we find in Matthew 1:21 *"And she (Mary) shall bring forth a son, and you shall call his name JESUS (Yeshua): for he shall save his people from their sins".*

To save is to preserve; to restore or to bring back to a former, original or normal condition of the soul. Therefore, Jesus Christ (Yeshua) preserves or restores our souls from the effects of sin.

John 1:12 *"But as many as received him (Yeshua), to them gave He power to become the children of God, even to them that believe on his name".*

The second mission of Yeshua is not yet consummated. It is the salvation/preservation/restoration of the body. Just as He has been able to preserve/restore our souls; Yeshua is able to preserve or restore our bodies for eternity so that both the soul and the body may live eternally with God.

110

Isaiah 61:2 speaks of the vengeance of the Lord as the second mission of Yeshua. Yeshua shall judge all those that will have rejected God's only means of salvation. Judgement is reserved until those that have accepted Yeshua have been taken away to glory together with both their souls and bodies. As of now, human beings are still in the grace of God which Isaiah refers to as "the acceptable year of the Lord".

After this period of grace comes the judgement of God as spoken of in Acts 17:31 *"Because he has appointed a day, in which he will judge the world in righteousness by that man (Yeshua) whom he has ordained; and of this he has given assurance unto all men, in that he has raised him from the dead".*

Bible scholars will be interested to take note that when Jesus Christ read from the book of Isaiah 61:1-2 in Luke 4:18-19, He omitted verse 2 which speaks of the vengeance of God because that was not within the scope of his first mission. When He comes for the second time, He is going to blow a trumpet to signal the resurrection of the dead in Christ and the transformation of the bodies of those who will be still alive but with faith in Christ. Both those who are dead and alive in Christ will meet Him in the air and be taken in a cloud to glory. They will be taken to go and have their deeds judged and rewarded. The following passages of scriptures will help summarise the events.

1 Corinthians 15:51-57 *"Behold, I show you a mystery; We shall not all sleep, but we shall all be changed, in a moment, in the twinkling of an eye, at the last trump: for the trumpet shall sound, and the dead shall be raised incorruptible, and we shall be changed. For this corruptible must put on incorruption, and this mortal must put on immortality. So, when this corruptible shall have put on incorruption, and this mortal shall have put on immortality, then shall be brought to pass the saying that is written, Death is*

swallowed up in victory. O death, where is your sting? O grave, where is your victory? The sting of death is sin; and the strength of sin is the law. But thanks be to God, who gives us the victory through our Lord Jesus Christ".

This is when the bodies of the righteous saints will be consummated in the preservation and restoration of the Lord. Death is what causes the flesh to perish. At the coming of Yeshua, "death is swallowed up in victory".

1 Thessalonians 4:16-17 *"For the Lord himself shall descend from heaven with a shout, with the voice of the archangel, and with the trump of God: and the dead in Christ shall rise first: Then we who are alive and remain shall be caught up together with them in the clouds, to meet the Lord in the air: and so, shall we ever be with the Lord".*

Hebrews 9:27-28 *"And as it is appointed unto men once to die, but after this the judgment: So, Christ was once offered to bear the sins of many; and unto them that look for him shall he appear the second time without sin unto salvation".* This verse is referring to the second coming of Christ when He is coming to preserve the bodies of the righteous saints.

When Christ (Yeshua) has preserved and restored the souls and the bodies of the righteous saints and has rewarded them for their good deeds; He will come back with them to earth as the military Messiah (Yeshua) together with the righteous saints as the army to fight for Israel and defeat its enemies. Satan and his demons shall be captured, chained and thrown into a bottomless pit for 1000 years and Christ together with the saints shall rule on earth in a peaceful kingdom for the same period.

After this millennium reign as it is called by bible scholars, Satan, and his demons and all the wicked dead shall be brought back for judgement to face the wrath and the vengeance of the Lord spoken of by Isaiah 61:2.

Revelation 20:11-15 *"And I saw a great white throne, and him that sat on it, from whose face the earth and the heaven fled away; and there was found no place for them. And I saw the dead, small and great, stand before God; and the books were opened: and another book was opened, which is the book of life: and the dead were judged out of those things which were written in the books, according to their works. And the sea gave up the dead who were in it; and death and hades delivered up the dead who were in them: and they were judged every man according to their works. And death and hades were cast into the lake of fire. This is the second death. And whosoever was not found written in the book of life was cast into the lake of fire".*

It is this second death that the righteous saints will have been preserved from by the Lord Jesus Christ. The righteous saints are the ones whose names are written in the book of life.

Jeremiah 17:13 *"O LORD, the hope of Israel, all that forsake you shall be ashamed, and they that depart from me shall be written in the earth, because they have forsaken the LORD, the fountain of living waters".*

The Lord preserves

God will be preserving the souls of his own. When he takes us out of danger, he will be preserving our souls. We may pass through the fire, but we shall not be burned because he will be preserving our souls.

When God is busy protecting his own, what actually will be happening is mysterious.

Isaiah 43:1-5 *"But now thus says the LORD that created you, O Jacob, and he that formed you, O Israel, Fear not: for I have redeemed you, I have called you by your name; you are mine. When you pass through the waters, I will be with you; and through the rivers, they shall not overflow you: when you walk through the fire, you shall not be burned; neither shall the flame scorch you. For I am the LORD your God, the Holy One of Israel, your Saviour: I gave Egypt for your ransom, Ethiopia and Seba in exchange for you. Since you were precious in my sight, you have been honourable, and I have loved you: therefore, will I give men for you, and people for your life. Fear not: for I am with you: I will bring your descendants from the east and gather you from the west".*

Through Isaiah the prophet, God was showing how he preserves his people from being destroyed by their enemies. God calls himself a "saviour" meaning that he saves or preserves. This is what King David understood when he penned Psalms 23:3 *"He restores my soul".* In the wake of this revelation, David made a prayer in Psalms 16:1 *"Preserve me, O God: for in you do I put my trust".*

King David put his trust in the Lord because he knew that the Lord preserved his soul from King Saul's attacks. When King David sinned and a prophet named Nathan came to condemn him, he repented and sought forgiveness from the Lord and the Lord preserved his soul.

2 Samuel 12:13 *"And David said unto Nathan, I have sinned against the LORD. And Nathan said unto David, The LORD also has put away your sin; you shall not die".*

Later, King David made this prayer of penitence:

Psalms 51:1-14 *"Have mercy upon me, O God, according to your loving-kindness: according to the multitude of your tender mercies blot out my transgressions. Wash me thoroughly from my iniquity, and cleanse me from my sin. For I acknowledge my transgressions: and my sin is ever before me. Against you, you only, have I sinned, and done this evil in your sight: that you might be justified when you speak, and be blameless when you judge. Behold, I was brought forth in iniquity, and in sin did my mother conceive me. Behold, you desire truth in the inward parts: and in the hidden part you shall make me to know wisdom. Purge me with hyssop, and I shall be clean: wash me, and I shall be whiter than snow. Make me to hear joy and gladness; that the bones which you have broken may rejoice. Hide your face from my sins and blot out all my iniquities. Create in me a clean heart, O God; and renew a right spirit within me. Cast me not away from your presence; and take not your Holy Spirit from me. Restore unto me the joy of your salvation; and uphold me with a free spirit. Then will I teach transgressors your ways; and sinners shall be converted unto you. Deliver me from the guilt of bloodshed, O God, God of my salvation: and my tongue shall sing aloud of your righteousness".*

After this prayer of penitence, the Lord preserved or restored the soul of King David. And in Psalms 23:3 David said, *"He restores my soul: he leads me in the paths of righteousness for his name's sake".*

King David could have lost his throne and favour of God through his sin of killing Uriah and taking his wife. But by repentance, asking for forgiveness and a prayer of penitence, God restored or preserved his soul. He trusted in the Lord and the Lord preserved his soul from perishing.

Joseph the son of Jacob told his brothers who had sold him to the Ishmaelites and was taken to Egypt that the Lord sent him ahead of time so that he may preserve lives.

Genesis 45:7 *"And God sent me before you to preserve you a posterity in the earth, and to save your lives by a great deliverance".*

God allowed Joseph to be sold into slavery to Egypt so that he could be the means by which God was going to preserve Jacob and the rest of his family from the hard-hit famine of Canaan.

With all the above-quoted accounts before King Solomon, he saw it fit to teach and instruct his son in Proverbs 3:5 to *"Trust in the LORD with all your heart; and lean not unto your own understanding".* He knew the promises of the Lord, the provision of the Lord and the preservation of the Lord.

Dead but raised back to life again – Oh! What a mystery?

Another of my testimonies that the Lord preserves life is as follows. In 1993, at Mutorashanga I had nausea and started vomiting. I became seriously ill and began to vomit green and black substances that were very smelly. The medical doctor at the Mutorashanga hospital failed to control and stop me from vomiting for two days. I could neither eat nor drink for the whole period. No medication was administered to me possibly because it was not yet necessary or too soon, I don't know the medical or clinical side of this. But my assumption is that I could have dehydrated and fainted with hunger. Albeit I remained alive.

By about 5.30 pm on the second day of my serious illness, my wife who had visited me at the Mutorashanga hospital bade me bye-bye hoping to visit me the following morning. I couldn't bid her farewell because it was very clear to me that in her early morning next visit, she was not going to see me on the bed in the same ward, but I could be in a mortuary, being counted amongst the dead. There was another super law that I understood at the time that prohibited me from disclosing to my wife that I was going away that night to be with the Lord.

I don't know at what time in the evening did I see my spirit leave my body into another spiritual realm. Immediately upon exit from my body, I saw myself ready to start on a very long journey. A voice spoke about a metre above my right ear, but I did not turn to see the voice that spoke to me. I am a Shona speaking person, but I was told in the English language, "Now, you are going to appear before the Most Supreme Being". I knew immediately that I was going to stand before the Almighty God and that I was going to give an account of how I had lived all my days on earth.

In the twinkling of an eye, I saw a very big and lengthy book like a bible opened about 100 metres wide. On the double pages across the book were strokes very close to each other from the day I was born to the day I died. Each stroke represented what was referred to as an ACT. Reading in the book, I understood clearly that an ACT is one piece of God's will over one's life. Any of the ACTS done constitutes a GOOD DEED before God and it is counted as RIGHTEOUSNESS. The so-called ACTS were innumerable but were meant to have been done in my lifetime.

In the spur of the moment, I was shown that I had the potential to have finished the ACTS within a very short time in my life based on the potential that was vested in me by the "Most Supreme Being" at birth.

I will illustrate. It's like being asked to sit for an examination paper that is scheduled for at least three hours but with the potential and speed that was vested in me, I had the ability to have finished in ten minutes a three-hour examination paper. Such was my potential and speed at which to execute my tasks.

Everything was moving so fast, and my result was revealed. I was shocked by the result, and I exclaimed loudly in despair. The result was embarrassing and shocking. I can't even at this time mention it. I was meant to take my results to the Most Supreme Being for determination and judgement. At that moment, I perceived within me that it was an insult to the holiness of the Most Supreme Being to appear before Him with such a shameful result. I had no excuse for such a poor result. I had no answer at all to give to the Most Supreme Being whom I was going to appear before.

I condemned myself immediately and judged and sentenced myself as deserving the stiffest of all punishments and that I should serve the punishment with joy though in great pain. God's holiness, majesty, awesomeness, glory, and justice is such that one judges oneself and determine for oneself where you want to spend your eternity. I determined my own fate in a split second. I didn't want to go and insult His holiness by coming to give an account because there was virtually nothing to account for.

Just to digress a bit. This incident happened at a time in my ministry when my wife and I thought that we had served the Lord faithfully and with all our hearts. We had witnessed God bring the dead back to life. We had seen God heal the sick and deliver the demon-possessed through us. We had seen God cause our Citroen GS Club to drive several kilometres in the Great Dyke Mountains of Mutorashanga on an empty tank (I testified about it earlier in this book). We had witnessed the abundant supplies of God when at one time, a certain Christian gathering unknown to us in the United States of America was told to send us suitcases of clothes for everyone in our family with correct sizes and they were sent to the correct address (I testified about it earlier in this book). Our preaching of the word was with much anointing. So, we consoled ourselves that indeed, we had served God, and should we die, we were to be accredited with greatness in heaven. And there I was now with a humiliating poor result.

In that moment of despair, disappointment and fear, the voice that previously spoke to me said, "I would like you to know that anything that is professionally done in the kingdom of God has no reward except that which is done according to His will no matter how simple and foolish it might be".

I learned immediately that all the work I had done and had earned me pride; had not been counted towards my ACTS. Possibly, I had done God's will, my way, and not His way. Possibly, it meant also that I had done God's will professionally as per my training and not according to His wisdom. I learned that God's work needs to be done according to His divine will and according to His divine ways and wisdom no matter how foolish His wisdom might appear to be.

Having understood these few great lessons, I immediately saw myself walking a very long journey back to my body which was displeasing to re-enter because of how filthy and unpleasant it looked. The distance I travelled back, indicated that; what I considered a split of a moment was a long-distance I had travelled. I re-entered my body and in less than 30 minutes my wife had come for an early morning 6.30 am visit. She found me seated and smiling on my hospital bed and completely well without any pain in my body. This was a divine miracle. It was a mystery as my name - Mystery.

The doctor's round came while my wife was still there; the doctor was surprised to see me well and seated. Without any further examination, he just said, "I can see you are well, and I must discharge you". I replied, "Yes! Doctor I am well. You can discharge me". He immediately discharged me from the hospital, and I walked about 4 kilometres to my residence unaided. The Lord preserved me from dying and restored my life because he had a plan and purpose for me to continue to do the work of ministry.

My wife on the night that I died had a sleepless night praying for me because of the condition she had left me in hospital. She came in the early morning visit hoping to see change because of her prayers. Indeed, there was change. She saw me awake, seated, well and smiling. God is faithful to the prayers of those that "trust in the Lord and lean not on their understanding". This is the fifth reason why The Lord should be trusted - He preserves.

SECTION 3: GOD CAN BE TRUSTED

CHAPTER 13: GOD CAN MEET OUR PSYCHOLOGICAL NEEDS

Psychological needs

According to Abraham Maslow's hierarchy of needs as previously stated in this book, people reach their highest moments of life when their needs have been fully satisfied. Some of these needs are psychological like the need to belong, to be loved, to be recognized and self-esteem. These needs provide intimate relationships, friendships, prestige, and feelings of accomplishments.

In the Lord Jesus Christ, I see all these psychological needs being met and Jesus making his adherents socially contented with life. A musical artist, Aretha Franklin had to sing a beautiful piece of lyrics entitled: *What a friend we have in Jesus.*

When I think in terms of my testimonies that I gave in the previous chapters, I can vouch to say that God can meet all my psychological, physiological, emotional, and spiritual needs. The Lord left me with a sense that I have a loving pastor and church; I have loving parents who cared for me; my wife who was just there for me and would not leave me

> **◉**
> She sang the song because she realised how Jesus fits into the equation of our lives and satisfy our physical, psychological, let alone spiritual and physical needs.

dying alone and my church folks who prayed for me. I felt a deep sense of belonging and love. My self-esteem was boosted by the support I received. I have found out that I can do almost everything through Christ who strengthens me [Philippians 4:13]. I have a peace of mind knowing that Christ gives me peace that surpasses every understanding and I have a community of believers in Christ who have a love for one another and will stand with me in times of hardships.

If Abraham H. Maslow states that a person can only be happy and can trust anybody who is able to meet their needs, so, I can safely say the Lord Jesus Christ deserves to be trusted because He can meet all the human needs.

CHAPTER 14: THE POWER OF THE LORD

The prophet Daniel understood the power that belongs to God almighty. Daniel 2:21-22 says, *"He changes times and seasons; he removes kings and sets up kings; he gives wisdom to the wise and knowledge to those who have understanding; he reveals deep and hidden things; he knows what is in the darkness, and the light dwells with him".*

In the scientific world that we are now living, we attribute changes to times and seasons to climate change and global warming. But Daniel understood that it is God who has the power to change the times and the seasons. God had declared in Genesis 8:22, *"While the earth remains, seedtime and harvest, cold and heat, summer and winter, day and night, shall not cease."* Until this day, nothing that the Lord declared in terms of times and seasons has ever changed.

In the modern world of democracy, we believe that people have a voice. They have power to set up governments and to remove them. Democracy is the rule of the people, by the people and for the people. But the Bible, through the mouth of the prophet Daniel, is very clear that it is God that has the power to remove kings and to set up kings.

King Nebuchadnezzar had a dream in Daniel 4:4-18 which none of the magicians, enchanters, astrologers and diviners were able to give an interpretation to. When Daniel came, he gave the interpretation in Daniel 4:24, "*this is the interpretation, O king: It is a decree of the Most High, which has come upon my lord the king, that you shall be driven from among men, and your dwelling shall be with the beasts of the field. You shall be made to eat grass like an ox, and you shall be wet with the dew of heaven, and seven periods of time shall pass over you, till you know that the Most High rules the kingdom of men and gives it to whom he will. And as it was commanded to leave the stump of the roots of the tree, your kingdom shall be confirmed for you from the time that you know that Heaven rules. Therefore, O king, let my counsel be acceptable to you: break off your sins by practicing righteousness, and your iniquities by showing mercy to the oppressed, that there may perhaps be a lengthening of your prosperity.*"

God gave King Nebuchadnezzar the dream to show him that it is God who has power to enthrone and dethrone kings. The King went ahead to ignore the advice given by Daniel the prophet that he should humble himself and repent from his sins and do what was right (Daniel 4:27). The Bible says in Daniel 4:29-31 that the King boasted of his greatness and prowess twelve months after the dream and its interpretation. In Daniel 4:33 it says, "*Immediately the word was fulfilled against Nebuchadnezzar. He was driven from among men and ate grass like an ox, and his body was wet with the dew of heaven till his hair grew as long as eagles' feathers, and his nails were like birds' claws*".

It doesn't do anybody good to disobey God and never to put your trust in Him. Nebuchadnezzar was removed from the throne until he humbled himself according to God's word that he was restored back his kingdom (Daniel 4:36-37).

In Daniel five, we have a similar account where Belshazzar, King Nebuchadnezzar's son misused God's temple utensils that were taken when they took captive the Israelites to Babylon. During his feast, he saw a handwriting on the wall which when interpreted by Daniel the prophet meant that his kingdom was weighed and found wanting and hence it was coming to an end. Daniel 5:30 tells us that the kings reign ended unexpectedly according to God's word.

When King Solomon was instructing his son in Proverbs 3:5-6, *"Trust in the LORD with all your heart; and lean not unto your own understanding. In all your ways acknowledge him, and he shall direct your paths"*, he was thinking in terms of God's power. He was instructing his son to trust in the power of the Almighty God who is the creator of heaven and earth. He knew that it is God who has the power to put someone to the throne and dethrone anyone whom He so pleases.

God can be trusted because He has power to remove people from thrones and to set up thrones for those He likes.

Possibly, he was thinking of his father King David how he had ascended to the throne and became king [1Samuel 16:1-13]. The Lord had told Samuel the prophet that He had rejected all the sons of Jesse that were present at the ceremony that none can be anointed to be king over Israel. When David was finally called, God confirmed to Samuel that he should arise and anoint him as King. David was enthroned to be King by God while Saul was being dethroned by God. So, King Solomon didn't want his son to underestimate the power of the LORD. He wanted him to understand that the best principle to respond to God is by putting your trust in Him. King Saul failed to establish his kingship by failing to fully obey God's word and to trusting in Him.

King Saul disobeyed God's word when he was told by Samuel the prophet to wait for him until he comes and offer sacrifices to the Lord before engaging in a battle. When he thought Samuel had delayed and possibly no longer coming, he offered sacrifices to the Lord himself against God's word.

1 Samuel 13:13-14, *And Samuel said to Saul, "You have done foolishly. You have not kept the command of the LORD your God, with which he commanded you. For then the LORD would have established your kingdom over Israel forever. But now your kingdom shall not continue. The LORD has sought out a man after his own heart, and the LORD has commanded him to be prince over his people, because you have not kept what the LORD commanded you."*

The second time, as if he had not learnt previous lessons to fully obey and trust the Lord with all his heart, King Saul in 1 Sam. 15:1-22 was instructed by the prophet Samuel to go and fight the Amalekites and annihilate everything. *"But Saul and the people spared Agag, and the best of the sheep, and of the oxen, and of the fatlings, and the lambs, and all that was good, and would not utterly destroy them: but everything that was despised and worthless, that they destroyed utterly"*-1 Samuel 15:9.

The prophet Samuel had to challenge the PRIDE that was growing in King Saul of thinking that he could do anything he thought was right without giving due diligence to God's word. *"...Because you have rejected the word of the LORD, he has also rejected you from being king"*– 1 Samuel 15:23.

Because of disobedience and failure to fully trust in the lord and never to lean on his own understanding, King Saul for the second time, was rejected as King of Israel by God.

Brethren in Christ, it comes with a heavy price to disobey God's word and fail to fully put our trust in the Lord but lean on our own understanding. It pays dividends to simply and fully obey and trust in the Lord. If we trust in the Lord,

It's just a blessing to trust the Lord.

we will experience his power, authority and protection.

One of the commands that Moses gave to the children of Israel in his long farewell address recorded in the book of Deuteronomy 18:9-14 said, *"When you are come into the land which the LORD your God gives you, you shall not learn to do after the abominations of those nations. There shall not be found among you anyone that makes his son or his daughter to pass through the fire, or that uses divination, or sorcery, or interprets omens, or is a witch, or casts spells, or is a medium, or a wizard, or consults the dead. For all that do these things are an abomination unto the LORD: and because of these abominations the LORD your God does drive them out from before you. You shall be perfect with the LORD your God. For these nations, which you shall possess, hearkened unto sorcerers, and unto diviners: but as for you, the LORD your God has not allowed you so to do".*

Leviticus 19:31 *"Regard not mediums, neither seek after wizards, to be defiled by them: I am the LORD your God".*

In view of the above scriptures regarding spirit mediums, we read of King Saul making his third error in 1 Sam 28:3-23. He consulted the spirit medium in disguise and asked to be brought the spirit of the prophet Samuel who had since died and buried. He did this to his demise.

It was in this backdrop that King Solomon advised his son in Proverbs 3:5, *"Trust in the Lord with all your heart and lean not on your own understanding. In all your ways, acknowledge the Lord".*

King Solomon knew that power belonged to the Lord. He knew too that like his father David who trusted in the Lord, he had ascended to the throne by God's grace in the midst of all his brethren. He knew how he became strong not by his own strength but by the grace of God. He knew first-hand, the benefits of trusting in the Lord in order to be powerful and famous. He knew that no armies ever stood against the power and wisdom of God in all generations of Israel.

King Solomon knew quite well that the lord has power:

    i.   To make one wise

    ii.   To make one rich

    iii.   To make one, strong and mighty in battle

    iv.   To provide for all the needs of his people

    v.   To preserve and protect those who trust in Him

    vi.   To guide safely through treacherous ways those that seek continually his face

It is true that the Lord has the power to protect from the hand of enemies those that trust in Him. The words of the prophet Isaiah in chapter 54 verse 17 says, *"No weapon that is formed against you shall prosper; and every tongue that shall rise against you in judgment you shall condemn. This is the heritage of the servants of the LORD, and their righteousness is of me, says the LORD".*

My Testimonies:

Indeed, the Lord protects, and no weapon formed or fashioned against His servants shall prosper. I come from a superstitious cultural African background that practices and believes in necromancers, *divination, sorcery, interprets omens, practices witchcraft, casts spells, consults spirit mediums and wizards, or consults the dead* as forbidden in Deuteronomy 18:10-11.

An evil omen in the flowerpot:

I remember one time my wife drove me and left me at a certain place that I was teaching, and she came back home with the car because she wanted to use it in the morning and was planning on picking me up later that day. While we were away, someone brought a beautiful flowerpot with a nice, beautiful flower plant and left it in our house. Someone had cast spells on the flowerpot that the moment either my wife or me touch it, we were immediately going to go mad and/or psychiatric.

When my wife arrived back home, she was told by our housemaid that a certain woman had brought us a flowerpot with a beautiful flower plant. As my wife was making steps towards the flowerpot, suddenly her mobile phone rung and she answered the call. This was her salvation from the Lord.

A prayer veteran woman by revelation during her prayer time had been revealed that in our home a woman had left a flowerpot with a beautiful plant. It had spells casts onto it to cause me or my wife to be psychiatric the moment we touched it. She advised my wife not to do anything with the flowerpot until I had come back home, and we had prayed on the phone with her so that we can then move it and thrown it away. My wife listened to the advice and when I came back, we prayed together with the prayer veteran woman and the Lord told us that it was safe for us to handle the pot and pour paraffin on it and burn the plant.

The Lord has the power to deliver anyone from any weapon that has been fashioned by the enemy against those who fear and trust in the Lord.

Nothing that the enemy envisaged to do in order to harm us ever materialised. The Lord had the power to destroy the magic powers of the enchanters, sorcerers and diviners.

God can be trusted because He has the power to deliver His people from the hands of their enemies. Even Daniel was delivered from the lions' den (Daniel 6:10-22). Paul and Silas were delivered from the prison (Acts 16:25) when they were praying. Peter was delivered from prison (Acts 12:4-11) when the church was praying for him.

Call for the heavens to stop the rain temporarily:

At one time, while I was pastoring at the Apostolic Faith Mission in Zimbabwe at God's Grace Centre (GGC), I was also the Regional Chairperson at that time; my church hosted a Regional Conference at Warren Park 1, Harare, Zimbabwe which was from Friday to Sunday. At that conference, there were so many people that were gathered to attend the Sunday morning service and clouds heavy with rains were hovering over our heads and people were not sheltered to prevent them from getting wet. I remember quite well that at about midday, I was preaching, and the rains were just about to fall. All I did was look at the sky and commanded the clouds to hold the rain until I finished preaching, and people have arrived at their homes. I continued to preach a very powerful sermon and I finished at about 1.30 pm and the leadership dismissed the people around 2.00 pm. According to my prayer and command, indeed, after 3.30 pm when everyone was at home, heavy rains fell down across the region for more than an hour.

God withheld the rains from pouring down while we were still at the conference because we trusted that our God could withhold the rains until His work was finished. Throughout my ministry, I learned to put my trust in the Lord with all my heart and never to lean on my understanding. In all my ways I have learned to acknowledge him, and He has always guided me.

Our God is an omnipotent, omnipresent and omniscient God. That means He is almighty and powerful; He is present everywhere at any time and He is all-knowing, and nothing hides in His sight. King Solomon understood this quite well and urged his dear son in Proverbs 3:5, "*Trust in the lord with all your heart and lean not on your understanding. In all your ways acknowledge Him*".

Saved from the mermaid:

In November 1981, my friends Philip Dambeni and Patson Kandare and I went on a preaching spree to Zambia from Zimbabwe. As young upcoming gospel ministers that believed in God's power, we went into all the four corners of Zambia preaching the gospel of our Lord Jesus Christ and declaring the power of God. Many miracles did happen during our preaching spree.

In our final week before Christmas, we went to preach in a nearby village to Mumbwa in Zambia, we wanted to conclude the crusade with water baptism before we left for Zimbabwe to celebrate Christmas at another crusade in Mamina, Mhondoro. We asked if there was a river nearby and we were told that there was a nice place nearby. We had eleven people that needed water baptism.

We organised ourselves to do baptism and asked people to bring their change of clothes. At the river, my friend Philip was to organise the people and instruct them on what to do when they got into the water since he was our interpreter. My friend Patson was to usher people into the water and to receive them after baptism. I was to go into the water to officiate the baptism.

To our surprise, when we arrived at the river there were already too many people from the nearby villages that had come to the baptismal site, and they were gathered on the other side of the river. We were not bothered, and we went ahead with our programme. I baptised the first giant man and he slipped off my hands and went under the water. I knew he was demon-possessed and so I never bothered. I called 2 or 3 more people and baptised them. Then resurfaced the man about 10 metres away from me. I re-immersed him into the water and again he slipped off. Again, I ignored and continued to baptise other people. He resurfaced about 5 metres away and I called him and baptised him again and this time he did not slip off but stood together with me as I prayed with him. He was immediately filled with the Holy Spirit and began to speak in other tongues. I left him speaking as I continued to baptise others and later, he left the waters.

As soon as he left the water, I saw an influx of people coming from the other side of the river wanting to be baptised. I didn't know whether my friend had preached to them in the other language or not, but I continued to baptise them all. We ended up baptising about 33 people instead of 11.

On the morrow we had a review of the baptism of the previous day. We all wandered how on earth we ended baptising more people than we anticipated. What we then learnt shocked us. Since we had been preaching about the power of God and that there is no other power greater than our God, the surrounding villages people wanted to see what powers we had that was greater than the power that they knew in the area.

FIGURE 3
MERMAID

Little did we know that the place that we conducted the baptism was a place that the locals knew was the place they often saw a mermaid. They did not tell us because they wanted to see how the mermaid was going to fight with us since we were going to invade its waters. Furthermore, nobody had bothered to alert us that among the candidates for baptism, there was a man who was used by the mermaids in necromancy. So, they had all come because they knew the giant man to be baptised was the one who was a mermaid medium.

Nobody had told me that if I had just made one more step further from where I stood baptising, I could have sunk into a deep pool which they believed was endless and that's where the mermaid lived. So, when they saw the man going under the water, they thought he had gone to call the mermaid. When he came out, they thought a mermaid was following to drown me and take me away forever. But when they saw me finish to baptise him and he came out of the water and I remained inside the water, they all believed that our God was indeed greater than the mermaid. That was the reason why they all wanted to be baptised. It was like the story of Paul at Malta in Acts 28:1-6 who when the venomous snake wound itself on his hand and he shook it into the fire, the local people thought he was a murderer, and he was going to die. When they saw that nothing happened to him, they changed their minds and said he was a god. So, we ended baptising more people because they had now believed in our gospel message about the power of God. We then had to ask the man of the mermaids to bring all the magic items and we burned them. The man later died, we were told, as an evangelist preaching the gospel and the power of God.

If I had just gone one step further, I could have drowned if it was not for God's power that restrained me from making another step into the deep. If I had just gone one step further, I could have been a fairy tale story of a man who boasted of a God who does not save but thank God, our God is powerful and has the power to save. If I had just gone one step further, my family could have missed me forever and they could not have known of the place of my disappearance, if it had not been of the power of God that sustained and preserved me. If I had just gone one step further, I could not have been alive today to write this book about trusting in the Lord.

> I trust in the Lord because I believe in the power of the Lord. It pays to trust in the Lord.

It was a mystery that I didn't take one step further into the deep. My name is Mystery and indeed it was a mystery that I survived by the power of God. My life from birth until now is a testimony of the power of God to preserve and protect my life. I agree with King Solomon that my son, trust in the Lord. There are awesome benefits in trusting in the Lord.

Amen.

Chapter 15: The Pathways of The Lord

The pathways of the Lord are always the right paths. They may seem to be dangerous and unsafe, but they are always the right paths. In Psalms 23:3, David said, *"...He leads me in paths of righteousness for his name's sake"*. It is for His own good reputation that the Lord leads his people in the paths of righteousness. In John 10:11, Jesus said, *"I am the good shepherd. The good shepherd lays down his life for the sheep"* as he protects them. In John 17:12, Jesus even confirmed to his Father in His prayer that He had not lost even a single sheep except the one who was predestined to be lost. The Lord deserves to be trusted because He leads in the right paths of righteousness so that He can attain for Himself a good reputation as a good shepherd.

David as a shepherd and knowing the goodness of the Lord over his life, he had to say in Psalms 23:4, *"Even though I walk through the valley of the shadow of death, I will fear no evil, for you are with me; your rod and your staff, they comfort me"*.

David knew quite well that some of the right paths of the Lord take you through the valley of the shadow of death. This was a valley that provided a short route between Jerusalem and Jericho parallel to the Jordan river. This route was not a safe route for travellers. This route could have been the route of the story that

Jesus talked about that man, who was attacked by robbers between Jerusalem and Jericho, and left half dead [Luke 10].

David metaphorically said that he took that route because of the comfort he got from the rod and staff in the hand of the good shepherd, the Lord. Had it not been of the trust he had in the Lord; he was not going to risk his life going the way of the valley of the shadow of death. There were so many incidences that David risked his life, but it was all because he trusted in the Lord. He fought with a lion and a bear and tore them apart by the beards, because he trusted in the Lord. He believed it was the Lord who was taking him to such challenging situations since he had been anointed to be king over Israel. His fight with giant Goliath was a risk to his life but he believed that it was God who took him to such a position to fight Goliath since he had been anointed to be king over Israel.

It was dangerous for him to minister before King Saul who on many occasions wanted to kill him by a sword, but he believed that it was God who would give him the grace to escape all the threats and dangers of King Saul. When he came before Doeg, king of Edom, he still believed that it was God who brought him to such circumstances so that he may learn that it is the Lord who is mighty to save. David understood that his ways are not God's ways, and his thoughts were not God's thoughts. So, all he did was trust God and follow him every moment of his life. He learned to commit all his ways to the Lord and to follow the pathways of the Lord.

All kings in Israel that walked in the pathways of the Lord enjoyed victories, successes, peace and rest from their enemies.

King Solomon knew quite well that all the victories of his father were a result of his trust in the Lord. He also knew that he was enjoying peace in Israel because he trusted in the Lord.

So, he wanted his son to walk in the pathways of the Lord so that he may be successful in all he does.

Three ways to please God:

In Micah 6:8 it says, He has told you, O man, what is good; and what does the LORD require of you (a) but **to do justice,** and (b) **to love kindness,** and (c) **to walk humbly with your God**? This is the pathways of the Lord.

Three things are essential in walking in the pathways of the Lord:

    i.   Justice

    ii.   Mercy/kindness

    iii. Humility

Trusting in the Lord helps us to do justice to other people. Justice is exercising fair and just treatment to other people. God is pleased with us if we treat others with the fairness they deserve. Justice is a fair and just application of God's law on God's people. Micah's argument in chapter six verses eight is that nothing pleases God except we act justly, and we love mercy, and we walk humbly with our God. God is not pleased with the amount of burnt offerings or anything we might give unless we exercise justice, mercy and humility. One of the pathways of the Lord is justice.

Another pathway of the Lord is mercy.

Mercy is defined by the Merriam Webster dictionary as compassion or forbearance that is shown especially to an offender or to one subject to one's power. It is also defined as leniency or compassionate treatment of other people. Others have defined mercy as not getting the punishment that you deserve because of love. If one trusts in the Lord, it means that one will be able to show mercy to those that need mercy. God is a merciful God and those that trust in Him should also show mercy to others. This was Jesus Christ's teaching in the parable of the unmerciful servant as quoted below:

"Therefore, the kingdom of heaven may be compared to a king who wished to settle accounts with his servants. When he began to settle, one was brought to him who owed him ten thousand talents. And since he could not pay, his master ordered him to be sold, with his wife and children and all that he had, and payment to be made. So, the servant fell on his knees, imploring him, 'Have patience with me, and I will pay you everything.' And out of pity for him, the master of that servant released him and forgave him the debt. But when that same servant went out, he found one of his fellow servants who owed him a hundred denarii, and seizing him, he began to choke him, saying, 'Pay what you owe.' So, his fellow servant fell down and pleaded with him, 'Have patience with me, and I will pay you.' He refused and went and put him in prison until he should pay the debt. When his fellow servants saw what had taken place, they were greatly distressed, and they went and reported to their master all that had taken place. Then his master summoned him and said to him, 'You wicked servant! I forgave you all that debt because you pleaded with me. And should not you have had mercy on your fellow servant, as I had mercy on you?' And in anger his master delivered him to the jailers, until he should pay all his debt. So also, my heavenly Father will do to every one of you, if you do not forgive your brother from your heart"- Matthew 18:23-35.

Jesus was emphasising the importance of showing mercy to others so that God may be merciful with us. Time and again, we are told in the bible that Jesus was always moved with compassion whenever He saw people.

Another pathway of the Lord is walking with humility with God. God resists the proud but loves the humble in heart. David was a humble man. Often, he would show remorse for his wrong actions if he knew them. He never wanted to intentionally offend God, but he was always quick to repent before God. To King Solomon, trusting in the Lord meant walking in the pathways of the Lord by acting justly, and loving mercy/kindness and walking humbly with the Lord our God. Such people always enjoyed the Lord's blessings, and he wanted his son to enjoy the same.

Our Christian failures:

Many times, as Christians we have failed to do as required in Colossians 3:12-14: *"Put on then, as God's chosen ones, holy and beloved, compassionate hearts, kindness, humility, meekness, and patience, bearing with one another and, if one has a complaint against another, forgiving each other; as the Lord has forgiven you, so you also must forgive. And above all these, put on love, which binds everything together in perfect harmony".* If we trust in the Lord, we will be able to

It pays to walk in the pathways of the Lord.

clothe ourselves with all these qualities that will help us to fulfil our moral duties to one another.

Amen

CHAPTER 16: THE PUNISHMENT OF THE LORD

There are serious consequences for failing to trust in the Lord and for leaning on one's understanding and failing to commit to the ways of the Lord. King Solomon knew what had befallen King Saul when he failed to trust in the Lord, and he leaned on his own understanding and failed to commit his ways unto the Lord. He did not want his son to, later on, walk in the footsteps of King Saul and end up being rejected and replaced by God.

There are few aspects about God that I would like to express. Nobody has set these principles for Him for there is none greater and above Him. He is His own master, and He governs Himself. He is a God of mercy, but His mercy is discretional.

> God is bound by who He is. He can't violate Himself. He functions within His set divine principles.

Exodus 33:19 says, *"...And I will be gracious to whom I will be gracious and will show mercy on whom I will show mercy".*

Romans 9:15 says, *"...I will have mercy on whom I have mercy, and I will have compassion on whom I have compassion." So, then it depends not on human will or exertion, but on God, who has mercy. For the Scripture says to Pharaoh, "For this very purpose I have raised you up, that I might show my power in you, and that my name might be proclaimed in all the earth." So, then he has mercy on whomever he wills, and he hardens whomever he wills (Romans 9:17-18).*

The punishment of the Lord is discretional based on the principle of mercy. First, let us define "Punishment". According to the Oxford dictionary – "It is the infliction or imposition of a penalty as retribution for an offence". So, punishment is justice being executed for an offence. Hence, punishment is something that is deserved by the offender. Mercy is defined by the Oxford dictionary as "compassion or forgiveness shown towards someone whom it is within one's power to punish or harm". So, it is one's prerogative to have compassion or forgiveness. This means that there must be sufficient evidence for discretional action.

Another part of God is that He is just. The justice of God demands that every offence must receive a corresponding punishment. But there is no justice without mercy. But mercy is discretional. So, God reserves the right to show mercy on whom He wants to show mercy. Therefore, there is no injustice with God.

If the offender does something pleasing to the offended, the offender might be shown some mercy when justice for the offence is being done. If one trusts in the Lord with all his heart and never leans on his understanding but commits all his ways unto the Lord; if peradventure he commits an offence, the Lord will reconsider his position and pardons him on the grounds that he trusts in the Lord. You may find mercy in the day you need mercy if you live a life of trusting in the Lord. It pays to trust in the Lord.

It is your lifestyle that invites mercy in the day you need mercy.

King Solomon knew very well that God sent Israel into exile as punishment for being idolatrous but each time they realised their mistakes and confessed their guilt and cried unto the same God for help, God was found to be merciful with them and He would deliver them from their oppressors. God's mercy was based on Israel realising her mistakes, confessing her guilt, trusting again in the Lord and crying out for help. This is why I say, mercy is discretional. So, it was wise that King Solomon shared with his son that the best way in life is simply to trust in the Lord so that you will have mercy on a day you need mercy.

1Kings 21:17-29 has the following interesting story:

"Then the word of the LORD came to Elijah the Tishbite, saying, "Arise, go down to meet Ahab king of Israel, who is in Samaria; behold, he is in the vineyard of Naboth, where he has gone to take possession. And you shall say to him, 'Thus says the LORD, "Have you killed and also taken possession?"' And you shall say to him, 'Thus says the LORD: "In the place where dogs licked up the blood of Naboth shall dogs lick your own blood."

Ahab said to Elijah, "Have you found me, O my enemy?" He answered, "I have found you, because you have sold yourself to do what is evil in the sight of the LORD. Behold, I will bring disaster upon you. I will utterly burn you up, and will cut off from Ahab every male, bond or free, in Israel. And I will make your house like the house of Jeroboam the son of Nebat, and like the house of Baasha the son of Ahijah, for the anger to which you have provoked me, and because you have made Israel to sin. And of Jezebel the LORD also said, The dogs shall eat Jezebel within the walls of Jezreel.' Anyone belonging to Ahab who dies in the city the dogs shall eat, and anyone of his who dies in the open country the birds of the heavens shall eat."

Ahab's Repentance

(There was none who sold himself to do what was evil in the sight of the LORD like Ahab, whom Jezebel his wife incited. He acted very abominably in going after idols, as the Amorites had done, whom the LORD cast out before the people of Israel.)

And when Ahab heard those words, he tore his clothes and put sackcloth on his flesh and fasted and lay in sackcloth and went about dejectedly. And the word of the LORD came to Elijah the Tishbite, saying, "Have you seen how Ahab has humbled himself before me? Because he has humbled himself before me, I will not bring the disaster in his days; but in his son's days I will bring the disaster upon his house."

The pathway of the Lord is a pathway of mercy based on being remorseful for one's sins. Ahab received mercy because he humbled himself before God and his punishment was deferred to a later time. James 4:6 says, *"God gives more grace, and He opposes the proud but gives grace to the humble."*

To avert God's punishment, one needs to trust in the Lord and be humble. This was King Solomon's advice to his dear son whom he loved to see prospering in his days.

Another aspect of God is His love. God is love. He treats His creation with love. Love seeks the highest good of another. God is always seeking the highest good of the other. This is why He exercises mercy and justice. Before, He does anything as punishment for sin, He normally sends a warning of an impending judgement. This is what He did to King Ahab in the story above.

146

When we read the story of the prophet Jonah when God wanted to bring judgement on Nineveh, God first had to send the prophet Jonah to deliver a message of the impending judgement. When the King heard the message, he put on sackcloth which is a symbol of humility in the Bible and instituted fasting in the land on the pretext that God was going to be merciful with them and relent from punishing them. Indeed, because of the King's humility and his nation, God relented from executing the punishment. God's love gives Him the patience to extend time on us so that within that time, we may do the right things so that He will have reason to exercise mercy.

When Jonah preached repentance on the streets of Nineveh, the capital of Assyria, the people responded and were spared. A century later, sometime between 663 and 612 B.C., Nahum preached in a time when Nineveh would not repent. Nahum's message revealed the nature of God.

Nahum 1:1-7 "The LORD is a jealous and avenging God; the LORD is avenging and wrathful; the LORD takes vengeance on his adversaries and keeps wrath for his enemies. The LORD is slow to anger and great in power, and the LORD will by no means clear the guilty. His way is in whirlwind and storm, and the clouds are the dust of his feet. He rebukes the sea and makes it dry; he dries up all the rivers; Bashan and Carmel wither; the bloom of Lebanon withers. The mountains quake before him; the hills melt; the earth heaves before him, the world and all who dwell in it.

Who can stand before his indignation? Who can endure the heat of his anger? His wrath is poured out like fire, and the rocks are broken into pieces by him.

The LORD is good, a stronghold in the day of trouble; he knows those who take refuge in him. But with an overflowing flood he will make a complete end of the adversaries and will pursue his enemies into darkness".

In His anger and wrath, He is swift to execute punishment on those who do wrong but *"He knows those who take refuge in him".*

"He knows those who take refuge in him" is the key point. Nobody can withstand the anger of God, not even the mountains and the seas nor the whirlwind but *"He knows those who take refuge in him".* This is why the advice is trust in the Lord. He will deliver you in the day of calamity because *"He knows those who take refuge in him".*

There are ten benefits that the psalmist mentioned in Psalms 91 that the Lord will reward to anyone who trusts in Him.

    i.   He will deliver you…

    ii.   He will cover you…

    iii.   His faithfulness will be your shield

    iv.   He will remove your fears.

    v.   No enemies will come near you

    vi.   No evil, no plague will come near you

    vii.   Guardian angels will be assigned on your side.

    viii.   He will answer when you call for help.

    ix.   He will bless you with long life.

    x.   He will show his salvation.

Failure to trust in the Lord will result in all these benefits being removed and the punishment will be severe.

Therefore, it pays to put your trust in the Lord. Psalms 103:13 says, *"As a father shows compassion to his children, so the LORD shows compassion to those who fear him"*.

CHAPTER 17: THE PROMOTION OF THE LORD

The Lord deserves to be trusted because He has power to lift up and power to set down. Psalms 75:6 says, *"For promotion cometh neither from the east, nor from the west, nor from the south…But God is the judge: he puts down one and sets up another. For in the hand of the LORD there is a cup, and the wine is red; it is full of mixture; and he pours out of the same"*.

The Lord's hand has a cup full of red wine to make glad those that trust in Him. Promotion always brings joy, peace and happiness. Daniel and his friends were filled with joy when God using King Nebuchadnezzar promoted them to Provincial Administrators in Babylon. God will always fight for His own and promote them in their lives.

Abraham was promoted to be great and blessed to be a father of the families on the entire earth. Joseph was promoted from being a prisoner to being a Prime Minister in Egypt second to Pharaoh. Joshua was promoted from being an armour bearer of Moses to a great leader of Israel. David was promoted from being an ordinary shepherd boy to a King of the united Israel. Esther an orphan was promoted to be the Queen in Babylon. Some disciples were fishermen but by divine calling they became fishers of men. Brethren, promotion is of the Lord for those that love Him.

God does not look at the outward appearance of a person when he wants to uplift him but looks at the heart. This is the message conveyed to Samuel the prophet by God when he was asked to go and anoint one of the sons of Jesse to be king in place of King Saul whom the Lord had rejected because of his rebellious attitude.

> *1Samuel 16:6-7 "And it came to pass, when they were come, that he looked on Eliab, and said, Surely the LORD's anointed is before him. But the LORD said unto Samuel, Look not on his countenance, or on the height of his stature; because I have refused him: for the LORD sees not as man sees; for man looks on the outward appearance, but the LORD looks on the heart".*

David who was not even considered to be anointed by Jesse and was not even there at the occasion was the one God wanted to be anointed to be king. Promotion comes from the Lord. God chose David because he was a man after his own heart. How did he become a man after God's own heart?

David trusted in the Lord. Even when he was just a shepherd boy, he trusted in the Lord. He learned to play musical instruments in the fields tending to his father's flock as he composed songs of praise and worship to God. He was a man of worship. God loves worship. God inhabits the praises of his people.

God does not negotiate with anyone as to who should be uplifted or not.

It is God who promotes and ordains people. God is sovereign and His will always prevail. Often, God makes known His will before time so that when things begin to happen, all will know that it is the Lord's doing. Allow me to talk about my beloved country – Zimbabwe.

The Nation of Zimbabwe

Sometime in the winter season in 1979 at the University of Zimbabwe, then Rhodesia, I attended a World Map Conference that was being hosted by Ralph Mahoney for the Acts Magazine. The conference is one of those most powerful and spiritual conferences that I have ever attended in my lifetime. On the last day of the conference, there were two prominent prophetic messages that were given about the Independence of Zimbabwe and the Voice of the African Women. For the purposes of this book, I will focus on Zimbabwe then Rhodesia.

A certain Pastor (name withheld because I can no longer locate him for consent to publication) spoke in an unknown Pentecostal tongue and another stood to interpret the tongues. The message was that the independence of Zimbabwe was imminent. The white settlers had nothing to fear because the man to be on the throne was going to have a reconciliation policy. This was at a time when whites were being killed in guerrilla warfare. It was also said that churches had nothing to fear because the same man was going to grant freedom of worship. This again was at a time when comrades (freedom fighters) were closing churches and Christianity was being labelled a white man's religion that disguised itself in letting the African land be taken by the white settlers.

However, the prophecy went further to say that first, there was going to be a new government formed by a white man and a black man. But this government was to last for a very, very, very, very, very short time. Indeed, there was an interim government of Bishop Abel Muzorewa and Ian Smith which only lasted about six months. After this came the ZANU PF led government by the late Prime Minister Robert Gabriel Mugabe with the late Canaan Sodindo Banana as President. The late Prime Minister's inaugural speech surprised the world. He announced a reconciliation policy and freedom of religion. Those policies are still on in Zimbabwe.

The same prophecy again said that the man with the reconciliation policy was going to be respected internationally and many nations were going to ask him to arbitrate on their national affairs and will be appointed head of many organisations. He was going to lead well his country for the first decade and he was going to call international friends to come and celebrate with him their tenth national independence. But after the tenth anniversary, the prophecy said that things were going to deteriorate as the government officials were going to begin to be corrupt. The economy was going to deteriorate into the fifteenth year and civil unrests was going to start from the 15th year and would get worse into the 20th year. By the 20th year, the government would fold hands and say, "we no longer have an answer to this". The prophecy continued that the man with the policy of reconciliation was only going to be removed by a sudden act of God, but churches were supposed to be praying and be united.

So, when God's word says, "trust in the Lord" it means that God may find favour with you and elevates you for his divine purposes.

What I wanted to illustrate is that it is God who ordains authorities. He promotes those whom He wants for his divine purpose whether for good or for evil. The election and inauguration of the late President RG Mugabe was ordained by God before people even thought that Zimbabwe was so close to having independence. The leadership that is ruling in Zimbabwe whether people may say it's good or bad, but the truth of the matter is, it was ordained by God.

King Solomon instructed his son to trust in the Lord because he knew that he was appointed to the throne of David by God.

> 1Chronicles 22:6-10 *"...David said to Solomon, "My son, I had it in my heart to build a house to the name of the LORD my God. But the word of the LORD came to me, saying, ...You shall not build a house to my name, because you have shed so much blood before me on the earth. Behold, a son shall be born to you who shall be a man of rest. I will give him rest from all his surrounding enemies. For his name shall be Solomon, and I will give peace and quiet to Israel in his days. He shall build a house for my name. He shall be my son, and I will be his father, and I will establish his royal throne in Israel forever.'*

However, inspite of God's word to King David, Adonijah the son of Haggith exalted himself and declared himself King when he saw that his father's health was frail.

> 1Kings 1:5-10, *"Now Adonijah the son of Haggith exalted himself, saying, "I will be king." And he prepared for himself chariots and horsemen, and fifty men to run before him. His father had never at any time displeased him by asking, "Why have you done thus and so?" He was also a very handsome man, and he was born next after Absalom. He conferred with Joab the son of Zeruiah and with Abiathar the priest. And they followed Adonijah and helped him. But Zadok the priest and Benaiah the son of Jehoiada and Nathan the prophet and Shimei and Rei and David's mighty men were not with Adonijah.*
>
> *Adonijah sacrificed sheep, oxen, and fattened cattle by the Serpent's Stone, which is beside En-rogel, and he invited all his brothers, the king's sons, and all the royal officials*

of Judah, but he did not invite Nathan the prophet or Benaiah or the mighty men or Solomon his brother".

When the news reached King David while he was on his death bed, he instructed that Solomon be anointed as King as per the Lord's word.

1Kings 1:33-35, *"And the king said to them, "Take with you the servants of your lord and have Solomon my son ride on my own mule and bring him down to Gihon. And let Zadok the priest and Nathan the prophet there anoint him king over Israel. Then blow the trumpet and say, Long live King Solomon!' You shall then come up after him, and he shall come and sit on my throne, for he shall be king in my place. And I have appointed him to be ruler over Israel and over Judah."*

It was very clear with King Solomon that man may have their own plans, but it is the Lord's will that always prevails. He could not have been king over Israel since Adonijah had already installed himself as king. It is the Lord who promotes even if others may be against it. One of the reasons why we should trust in the Lord is that the Lord promotes those that trust in him, and the Lord will protect them from their enemies.

In closing brethren, I say it pays to trust in the Lord. It's a principle to responding to God. God earned the trust by the things he did and He deserved the trusted for who He is and He can be trusted for what He is capable of doing.

Endnotes

---

[i] https://www.britannica.comA/biography/Abraham-H-Maslow

[ii] https://www.linkedin.com/pulse/biblical-view-maslows-hierarchy-needs-david-shock. A Biblical view of Maslow's hierarchy of needs, published on March 9, 2015 by David J Shock, MA, LMHC.

[iii] https://www.nytimes.com/2017/01/12/nyregion/new-york-today-martin-luther-king-sneeze-izola-ware-curry-ive-been-to-the-mountaintop-speech.html#:~:text=in%20interstate%20travel.%E2%80%9D-,%E2%80%9CIf%20I%20had%20sneezed%2C%20I%20wouldn't%20have%20been,dream%20that%20I%20had%20had.%E2%80%9D

Printed in Great Britain
by Amazon